# WISHWOOD REVISITED

A New Interpretation of T.S. Eliot's
*The Family Reunion*

# WISHWOOD REVISITED

A New Interpretation of
T.S. Eliot's
*The Family Reunion*

Giles Evans

Foreword by
Lyndall Gordon

The Book Guild Ltd
Sussex, England

*To Lisabeth and Miriam*

The Book Guild Ltd.
25 High Street,
Lewes, Sussex.

First published 1991
© Giles Evans 1991
Extracts from T.S. Eliot's unpublished letters
on pages 16, 122 & 135 Valerie Eliot 1991

Set in Baskerville
Typesetting by Southern Reproductions (Sussex)
East Grinstead, Sussex.
Printed in Great Britain by
Antony Rowe Ltd.,
Chippenham, Wiltshire.

British Library Cataloguing in Publication Data
Evans, Giles 1949-1988
Wishwood Revisited: a new interpretation of T.S. Eliot's
'The Family Reunion.'
1. Drama in English. Eliot, T.S.
I. Title
822.912

ISBN 0 86332 573 4

# CONTENTS

| | | |
|---|---|---:|
| Acknowledgements | | 6 |
| Foreword | | 8 |
| Preface | | 9 |
| Chapter One | Critical Introduction | 13 |
| Chapter Two | Mary | 25 |
| Appendix to Chapter Two | | 47 |
| Chapter Three | Agatha and Amy | 51 |
| Chapter Four | The Uncles and Aunts | 66 |
| Chapter Five | Harry and Agatha | 83 |
| Chapter Six | The Effect on Amy and Mary of Harry's Departure | 105 |
| Chapter Seven | 'Under Compulsion of What Experience . . .?' | 120 |
| Chapter Eight | A Matter of Form and Performance | 132 |
| | I The Eumenides | 134 |
| | a) Classical and Modern | 135 |
| | b) Visible or Invisible? | 137 |
| | c) Spiritual Revelation | 141 |
| | d) Supernatural and Natural | 145 |
| | II The Chorus | 150 |
| | III Verse | 153 |
| | IV Conclusion | 167 |
| Bibliography | | 171 |
| Notes | | 175 |

# ACKNOWLEDGEMENTS

The Author and The Book Guild Ltd. wish to thank Faber and Faber Ltd. for their permission to reproduce extracts from the following works: *The Family Reunion, The Cocktail Party, 'Choruses from "The Rock" ', from Collected Poems 1909-1962, Selected Essays* and *On Poetry and Poets* by T.S. Eliot. Also extracts from *The Family Reunion with Introduction and Notes* by Nevill Coghill and *T.S. Eliot's Social Criticism* by R.J. Kojecky. We wish to express special appreciation to Mrs Valerie Eliot for permission to reprint three passages from hitherto unpublished letters, and these extracts appear on pages 16, 122 and 135 of this book.

Our thanks are also due to the authors and publishers with whose permission quotations are reproduced in this study and in particular to the following: to the Cambridge University Press for passages from *The Making of T.S. Eliot's Plays* by E. Martin Browne, from *Two in One* by E.M. & H. Browne, from *The Dark Comedy* by J.L. Styan, from *Six Dramatists in Search of a Language* and *Dramatic Dialogue* by A. Kennedy, from *Thomas Stearns Eliot, Poet* by A.D. Moody: to the Princeton University Press for quotations from *The Third Voice* by D. Donoghue: to Routledge for quotations from *Drama and Reality* by R. Gaskell and from *The Plays of T.S. Eliot* by D.E. Jones: to Chatto and Windus for quotations from *The Living Principle* by F.R. Leavis and from *Drama from Ibsen to Eliot* and *Drama from Ibsen to Brecht* by R. Williams: to Macmillan for quotations from *Eliot and the Living Theatre* by Katharine Worth (in *Eliot in Perspective* ed. C.G. Martin): to Hodder and Stoughton for quotations from *In My Mind's Eye* by M. Redgrave: to Methuen for quotations from *Building a Character* by C. Stanislavsky: to the Athlone Press for quotations from *Irish Drama from Yeats to Beckett* by Katharine Worth: to Hamish

Hamilton for quotations from *T.S. Eliot* by Peter Ackroyd: to the Oxford University Press for quotations from *Eliot's Early Years* by Lyndall Gordon: to Pitman Publishing for quotations from *Drama in Performance* by R. Williams: to the editors of *The Times, The Times Literary Supplement, The Guardian* and *The Illustrated London News* for quotations from reviews which appeared in their respective journals. Full details of all books and articles from which quotations have been taken can be found in the bibliography at the end of this volume.

# FOREWORD

In 1987, Giles Evans came to lunch at St Hilda's College, Oxford, where we had a long and, I felt, useful discussion about T.S. Eliot's plays on which we were both, at the time, working. We agreed that *The Family Reunion*, which had little success in Eliot's lifetime, had yet to be fully recognised as the most profound, poetic, and searching of the plays. We wondered if Eliot had possibly under-rated the capacity of a secular audience to tolerate the non-realistic elements in the play, so that his director, E.Martin Browne, had instituted the common staging which hides the Furies in a side window. We spoke admiringly of Michael Elliott's Royal Exchange production in 1979 where the insubstantiality of reported phantoms is confounded by a dramatic shock when they enter.

After this meeting, Giles Evans sent me an unfinished draft of the book he was writing on this play. I sent back pages of suggestions for revision; then, some time after, heard from Mrs Evans that he was too ill to do anything further. I was glad to hear of its publication, and am sure that it will be of immense use to teachers and future directors of *The Family Reunion*.

Lyndall Gordon,
Oxford, April 1990.

# PREFACE

Of the many people who are fascinated by the theatre few are equally captivated by T.S. Eliot. Yet Giles Evans was such a one. Though his compelling interest in Eliot's work was understandably a later development, the theatre had enchanted him since boyhood. During the last dozen years of his life these two preoccupations had an equal hold on him. It is not surprising, therefore, that anything that he might write about an Eliot play should proceed from an imagined performance, and that any analysis he might make would be aimed at enabling an actor playing in it to understand what he was saying and doing more fully. To enter more deeply and completely into the complex of human experience that constitutes the play is the end to which his study of *The Family Reunion* is directed.

I do not know exactly when Giles's interest in T.S. Eliot began but I'm pretty sure that his interest in Eliot *as a dramatist* dated from the time he spent working at the Chichester Festival Theatre in 1968, between leaving Westminster School and going up to Oxford to read English. He was employed as dresser to the three leading actors of the season, Sir John Clements, Peter Ustinov and Sir Alec Guinness, the last playing at that time in a production of Eliot's *The Cocktail Party*. These few months were of enormous importance in Giles's life. They intensified the spell which the theatre exercised over him by enabling him to be involved in it and to see it from an unusual angle, they brought him into very close contact with Eliot the dramatist, and they gave birth to his subsequent feeling that Sir Alec Guinness is the *non pareil* among actors. Seeing *The Cocktail Party* (or at least large parts of it) so many times opened his eyes to the depth and density of the play and hence to his feeling that, whatever the received critical

9

opinion of Eliot as a dramatist may be, he was one who had much to say to him and one who would both stimulate and repay thought. After these few heady months at Chichester, Oxford was something of an anticlimax, and Giles came to feel that his time there may have been a mistake. On the evidence of this book I do not think that he was right about that.

My own acquaintance with him began when he arrived as student teacher in my department at King Edward's School, Birmingham, in the school year 1971-72, but it was not until several years later, in 1975, after I had managed to lure him back to King Edward's School on a permanent basis, that we began to know each other well. I recollect the enthusiasm with which he greeted an off-the-cuff remark of mine to the effect that, however we finally judge the overall artistic success of *The Cocktail Party*, it is impressive as a penetrating study of the abrasive tensions that can wreck a marriage and that as such it is worth studying. The implication that the play might benefit from being treated as a play about people rather than as a semi-allegorical homily about the way to salvation obviously struck a responsive chord in him. The goal of the second of these possible approaches might be most satisfactorily attained by following the first. This is certainly how he has gone about his treatment of *The Family Reunion* where, in his characteristically patient and determined way, he has explored the play's main characters and the subtext of their lives to arrive at a profound understanding of the play's overall meaning.

When Giles began to study Eliot's dramatic writings systematically I do not think that *The Family Reunion* constituted a special focus of interest. He had directed a production of *Murder In The Cathedral* at school, and in 1982 he used a sabbatical term to work on *The Rock* and to write a substantial and, as yet unpublished, essay on it. Then, in 1984, he devised and tutored a week's residential course at Dillington College, Somerset, which explored Eliot's drama through workshops. He and his adult students worked on particular scenes from various plays, including some from *The Family Reunion*. It was possibly from this point that his attention began to focus particularly on this play. He felt that although it was the most problematical of Eliot's five dramatic ventures, a view that few would have questioned, it was also the most profound and could be seen as his most important contribution to drama. For the three years after 1984 he pursued his researches on the play while at the same time leading the busy life of a teacher with its heterogeneous demands on time and energy, directing plays, supervising the building of a drama studio and organizing many dramatic projects both within and without the school. By the autumn of 1987 he had finished the first draft of his study of *The Family Reunion*. A few weeks later he became aware of the illness which was subsequently diagnosed as a malignant spinal tumour.

During the eight or nine months between the diagnosis of his illness and his death in August 1988 the future of this book was seldom far from his mind. Although in this period he was engaged in the desperate and ultimately losing battle against cancer, and although he also wrote and delivered a substantial talk on *Drama and Liturgy,* he was constantly concerned with what he saw as the problem of how best to get his work on *The Family Reunion* into print. He was aware of practical considerations that might make publication difficult. He knew that his book was an awkward length – rather short for a major critical study and yet too long for an essay or an article. On the one hand he had been advised that he might do well to consider condensing its argument to the length of a substantial article for an appropriate periodical and on the other to try his luck at publishing it as it stood. Doubts had also been expressed about the nature and identity of its intended readership. It had been suggested that *The Family Reunion* itself was not popular enough to qualify this study for inclusion in any of the series of critical studies that aim at a student readership. Moreover, the point had been made that, dealing as it does with only one play, its scope was too narrow for the general reader while its method was too ponderous for the professional academic who does not need points to be established with the painstaking thoroughness that this book displays. Giles was the first to acknowledge the force of these considerations, and it was the problem of what to do about them that occupied him a good deal during his illness. In the last few weeks of his life he began to construct a condensed revision of the first chapter, in which he was greatly helped, as he had been all along, by his wife, Lisabeth.

Although Giles was envisaging the possibility of distilling the material of the book to the length of an article, this was not a task that I felt competent to attempt and have preferred to follow the alternative advice, namely, to seek publication of the original draft. It was, therefore, particularly gratifying when The Book Guild agreed to publish the book as it stood. There is no doubt that Giles would have revised it in some way but I do not know how or to what extent. Consequently I have made no attempt to retrench the material or to alter its arrangement and have confined myself to clarifying and tightening the expression where it was occasionally loose and could be improved.

I know that Giles would wish to record his thanks to the many people whom he consulted during his work on the play and who helped him with information and opinion on various matters. In the first place there are those in the theatre who had been in some way or other connected with the play – Mrs Stella Mary Newton, Miss Eileen Atkins, Sir John Gielgud, Sir Alec Guinness, the late Sir Rex Harrison, Mr Edward Fox and Mr Paul Scofield. In the second place there are those who knew T.S. Eliot – the late George Every and Mrs Valerie Eliot, who was able to direct him to some collections of material in America. Finally there are those who read Giles's draft and made many helpful and encouraging comments on it – Professor Katharine Worth, Professor John Creaser and Dr Lyndall Gordon, who has very kindly written a foreword to this book. Giles would have been absolutely delighted with that.

Anthony Trott
Birmingham, 1990.

# 1

## Critical Introduction

My intention in these pages is to meet the challenge offered by a certain line of criticism of T S Eliot's writing, namely that he was a major poet, but what a pity he was a Christian; his humanity is marred by the penitential nature of his religion. Such a view derives from those of Eliot's contemporaries who felt that he had done something not quite respectable in becoming an Anglican in 1927. He had betrayed those who looked to him as a guide from the waste land of post-war disenchantment. He had seemed to be speaking for a generation; then he abandoned his people. The uneasiness of many critics with Eliot's Christianity lies in their feeling that he sells short this world – the world of human beings and human relationships – in favour of another world, the heavenly kingdom which seems to exclude the love of created beings. Thus, for instance, F R Leavis grows uncomfortable when he comes to *Four Quartets*.[1] He finds these the expression of 'human nullity', and sees a contradiction between the poet who inherits the language developed through the human community of artists, and the same poet who denies value to the life of humanity.

Focusing on the plays  rather than the poems, Ronald Gaskell[2] gives an interesting analysis of *The Family Reunion* and alludes to *Murder in the Cathedral*. However, he concludes that 'between the natural (biological) life of man and the ethical or religious life Eliot can see no relationship'. Eliot is a 'dramatist uninterested in the natural world' who none the less tries, in *The Family Reunion*, to write naturalistically. Gaskell points to a dualistic vision separating body and spirit. 'The natural world is left to establish itself through the physical presence of the actors; and since there is no significant physical action in the play, this world is simply not made real for us – real to our imagination'. If indeed such dualism prevents Eliot from giving flesh to his characters this would seem to be a fundamental disqualification for a dramatist. J L Styan in *The Dark Comedy*[3] gives a sympathetic analysis of ironies present in the contrasting levels of reality and of values in the plays. Nevertheless, he concludes '(Eliot) could never make his prosaic people strong enough to withstand the imaginative assault of his more spiritual heroes and heroines; he seemed unable to grant them a philosophically justifiable and theatrically demonstrable value in their own right'. Of the Uncles and Aunts in *The Family Reunion*, Styan uses the words 'lesser mortals', unable to live on several planes at once. In *The Cocktail Party*, Celia is felt to outstrip the rest of the field and, even after she is dead, her unseen presence dwarfs the merely 'banal plodders'.

The view of *The Family Reunion* which sees Harry and Agatha as characters of perception isolated from a cast of shallow and interfering relatives, inadequate in the face of the mysterious and supernatural, seems to be repeated in several criticisms of the play. Denis Donoghue[4] feels that Eliot's language divides the characters into groups rather than creates individuals. These groups are not held in an adequately dramatic tension within the play. There is no balance of give and take; rather Harry, representing conscience and consciousness, is driven by divine agents to repudiate and destroy Amy's world of domesticity. Donoghue feels that the poet's voice reinforces this approach to the play; Eliot himself is too often heard where we ought to be hearing the characters speaking. In Donoghue's view of the play the action really ends after Harry's 'I shall be safe with them; I am not safe here'. Harry has passed through his private crisis and the last part is formally redundant; Amy dies, but there is nothing 'essential to the dramatic pattern'.

Even in his seminal and sympathetic analysis of the plays, D E Jones[5] comments that the function of the main chorus in *The Family Reunion* is to represent 'obtuse humanity'. Furthermore he argues that 'the fact that the central character exists in a world of his own, quite distinct from the world of most of the others in the play, is apt to hamper dramatic movement'.

Many people feel that they are asked by Eliot to see Harry's way as the right way and to denigrate the quality of life exhibited by the other characters. If the play does fall out like this Eliot may, with some justice, be accused of spiritual snobbery. However A D Moody's[6] comments on the play are more merciful, because he treats Eliot's spiritual development with sympathy. Even then, he sees *The Family Reunion* as a fascinating stage in the progress of Eliot's *poetry* towards *Four Quartets*, rather than as a play to be experienced live in the theatre: it is better as a radio play, he feels. For him, the play shows Harry to have achieved his destination at the moment of illumination. For the enactment of his new life, the spiritual action, we have to go on to the last three of the Quartets. Harry's insight is into a sense of sin and purgation. This, Moody argues, is not merely a personal insight but an acknowledgement of a fallen world in need of redemption; this acknowledgement must be at the root of Eliot's 'Christian Society'. This elucidation of the play in terms of Eliot's social theology seems to me exact as far as it goes. However, the focus in Moody's analysis is still on Harry as the special being, and not on the dramas of Mary or Amy. The Uncles and Aunts are seen as stock figures of the theatrical country house, representing the unreality and banality of a life made up of illusions. It seems that, faced with Eliot's plays, many literary critics seem compelled to schematise.

Related to the supposed duality in Eliot's philosophy and characterisation in *The Family Reunion* is a criticism on the more technical level. Eliot, we are told, confuses his styles. In his attempt to suggest the reality of a spiritual dimension in everyday life, Eliot resorts to non-naturalistic devices in an otherwise naturalistically conceived play. The Choruses, the Furies, and the moments of intense poetry are the offenders. Such is the reservation about the play made by Warren Harris[7] in a doctoral dissertation on Eliot's theatrical style. He sees *The Family Reunion* as a major step in Eliot's progress away from a 'formalised' style towards the naturalism of *The Cocktail Party* and *The Confidential Clerk*. These later plays show Eliot writing for the theatre as he really wanted to. In *The Family Reunion* he hadn't quite settled his style, but he had broken away from the liturgical style favoured by his producer, Martin Browne.

Despite this critical reservation, Harris's approach to the play is most suggestive and positive. He analyses the details of Eliot's craft in terms of transition from 'non-illusory', 'formal' theatrical presentation to a 'naturalistic', 'representational' text and staging. It is a suggestive approach because it considers aspects of the plays as texts for performance, but it is an approach limited by the theoretical framework: the distinction between 'naturalistic' and 'formal' suggests too restrictive a view of how theatre communicates in practice.

Such criticisms of *The Family Reunion* as we have been discussing are really extensions of the doubts Eliot himself expressed about the value of the play. Writing twenty years after the first production[8] he sensed an awkwardness in how the Aunts and Uncles speak both as individuals and as chorus. The verse in the two aria passages involving Harry and Mary and Harry and Agatha he felt to be 'beyond character', when they ought to have arisen naturally from character and situation. He felt he had not developed the action of the play which he had so carefully set up in the opening scenes. The Furies, he felt, failed completely because the Greek and the modern conventions were not properly fused. Finally, he came to see Harry as an 'insufferable prig'. Even before 1951 Eliot had felt that Harry's state of mind and the nature of his illumination were not sufficiently objectified, and that the problem was not solved by the Furies.[9] The criticism he had made of Hamlet applied to his own play; there was no objective correlative adequate to the protagonist's state of mind. Most radically, by 1951 Eliot felt that there was a disastrous confusion in the response the play evoked: we do not know whether to consider the play 'the tragedy of the mother or the salvation of the son'. Eliot's sympathies came to be 'all with the mother', who seemed to him, 'except perhaps for the chauffeur, the only complete human being in the play'. If Harry *is* an insufferable prig, the play crumbles, unless, that is, there is a consistent way of looking at the play which can accommodate Harry's priggishness. The traditional reading that the play sides with Harry and his illumination against the half-life of other characters, needs to be questioned. Furthermore, if the apparent supremacy of Harry is seen to be qualified within the drama itself, the way is open to challenge those who find Eliot inhumane.

Kristian Smidt[10] opens up a new area of appreciation, namely the positive influence of Ibsen on *The Family Reunion*. Smidt gives an account of the way Eliot's view of Ibsen changed, at first seeing him through the social realist spectacles of Bernard Shaw, but later appreciating him as a finer poetic dramatist in prose than even Yeats in verse. In 1954 Eliot is published as saying that he had 're-read Ibsen's plays'[11], and Smidt records a personal conversation in 1948 when Eliot said, 'I read Ibsen's plays consecutively to work myself up before writing *The Family Reunion*, but reading them all together I cannot tell what impressions have subconsciously affected me'. Without wishing to make any one play a dominant influence, Smidt brings out compelling parallels between Eliot's play and *Rosmersholm, Ghosts* and, most strikingly, *John Gabriel Borkman*. The puzzle Martin Browne expressed about why the play should be set in a north-country mansion[12] becomes explicable when one thinks of the cold mansions of Norway that form the settings of Ibsen's plays of contemporary life. Smidt's summary of the affinities is worth quoting:

> 'The explorations of hidden relations in a family seen more or less in isolation from the outside world, the indefinable guilt and the revelation of the past which clarifies, punishes and liberates, all these are common features that Eliot could have taken over from Ibsen, though they were by no means Ibsen's monopoly.'

Smidt takes the discussion deeper by suggesting that the poetic quality that Eliot came to acknowledge in Ibsen lay in the importance of Aristotle's *anagnorisis* or 'recognition': 'the change from ignorance to knowledge, producing love or hate between persons destined for good or bad fortune' is an important feature of Ibsen's plays. Eliot, it is argued, achieves this kind of 'recognition' to admirable effect in *The Family Reunion*, but he moves away from it too soon in the plays which follow. If Eliot did not achieve quite enough of Ibsen's realism in *The Family Reunion*, he did surpass Ibsen in another respect. In *Borkman* the moral conflict lacks a spiritual dimension which makes sense of happenings, which on the purely human level are senseless: 'in Eliot's play events have a different and more meaningful pattern in addition to that of ordinary cause and effect'. It seems to me essential to Smidt's tribute that he sees Eliot's spiritual dimension as an *addition to,* not a replacement of, ordinary cause and effect.

I have paused to consider Smidt's published lecture at some length because it provides an authoritative analysis which reinforces what *The Family Reunion* has increasingly suggested to me in performance and study: that it is in considering the play as a drama in the tradition of Ibsen and of Chekhov that it yields its theatrical richness.

Another and independent linking of Eliot with Ibsen is made by Andrew Kennedy.[13] Where Smidt speaks of 'recognition', Kennedy explores the dramatic technique of the 'confessional duologue'. He is cautious in ascribing awareness on Eliot's part of affinities with Ibsen; Smidt, however, encourages us to be confident of these, and thus it will be fruitful to pursue the notion of 'confessional duologue' in Eliot's plays further than Kennedy feels possible.

Kennedy points to the innovative nature of the confessional duologue in Ibsen, which we see at its most accomplished in the structure of *Ghosts* and *Rosmersholm*.[14] The dramatic movement is towards deeper communication. The preparations he describes as 'tremors' before eventually the 'taboo on speech' is broken and clarity is gained with true understanding of the past and of the characters. The duologue has naturalistic form but goes deeper than 'imitation' of ordinary conversation: 'a gradual intensification, a layer-by-layer movement from the periphery to the centre, colloquial speech converted into dramatic poetry'[15]. Kennedy suggests that Eliot experimented in this kind of writing, and gives as paradigms Harry and Mary, Harry and Agatha and Celia in Reilly's waiting room (sic). Evasive speech yields at dramatic moments to real communication: 'the point where two characters lead one another to make a discovery – to understand the past – to clarify identity – *through* talk'. From *The Family Reunion* Kennedy only discusses the Harry-Mary duologue, and this restriction of the analysis is a major limitation on the effectiveness of his approach in an otherwise stimulating discussion of Eliot's search for a dramatic language. For him, the Mary duologue eventually fails because Eliot also calls upon other methods of intensifying speech which are a stylistic confusion of the 'conversational model' of Ibsen. He cites Harry's recourse to Eliotic language ('The aphyllous branch ophidian'), the trance-state duet and the appearance of the Eumenides – these last two reiterating Eliot's own objections.

Kennedy unfortunately limits the effectiveness of his discussion of the confessional duologue in *The Family Reunion* in three ways. First, Celia with Reilly in *The Cocktail Party* is not an equivalent of Harry with Mary or Agatha. Neither of these women has Reilly's professional detachment in the duologues; both are personally involved with Harry's search for identity and purpose – Mary as the one hoping to marry him, Agatha as one crucial in the guilty past of the family. Secondly, and following from this confusion, Kennedy tends to see the Eliotic duologue as an intimate exchange between a confessor (or confidant) and the protagonist, who needs to lessen the burden of past experience in order to reveal his true identity and purpose. This may be true of Celia, but an analysis of Agatha and Harry in duologue shows the more Ibsenesque pattern. Agatha needs Harry as a confessor just as much as he needs her as a confidante, and the scene dramatises a mutual unburdening of past experience. Kennedy falls victim to the schematisers when he sees Agatha as the 'quasi-priestess' and, by implication, misses her humanity. Finally, Kennedy does not refer to the duologue of Amy and Agatha, which focuses the confrontation of two women who break the taboo on speech after many preparatory tremors through the play. The duologue here is a tragic one, and it displays none of the objections that Kennedy raises about the Mary-Harry duologue. Perhaps it is not confessional enough to fit Kennedy's criteria, but it shows Eliot perhaps at the height of his dramatic powers. It was of this encounter that David Jones made an early hint in a footnote, that Ibsenesque technique was at work in the play.

The illuminating line of inquiry opened up by these links with the dramaturgy of Ibsen may be developed further in connection with Eliot's professed debt to Chekhov. In a letter to Geoffrey Faber in March 1937 Eliot stresses the gloom of *The Family Reunion*, and says that perhaps he's been influenced by Chekhov. Eleven months later he is much more open to Mrs Faber: 'The tragedy, as with my Master Chekhov, is as much for the people who have to go on living, as for those who die'. Amy, he confirms, is the only one who dies. Nevill Coghill[16], who quotes these two extracts in his introduction to the play, goes on to suggest how Eliot christianises Chekhovian elements such as the country house over which there broods 'a sad sense of futility and doom', where heart-break is balanced by 'hilarious touches of human comedy', and all is 'natural and spontaneous and truthful'. It may be disputed whether the humour, residing mainly in the Uncles and Aunts, is really Chekhovian in its timbre, although it does at times comically place the impending tragedies of the main plot in a Chekhovian balance. Rather it is, Eliot claims, the gloom that connects the play with Chekhov. On present information we can only speculate on whether Eliot saw any of Komisarjevsky's productions of Chekhov in London in the 1920s and 30s. These productions tended to lighten the supposed gloom and bring out the humour.

A more important indication from Eliot's comment is that at this time he saw beyond the tragedy of the mother who dies, and beyond the salvation of the son to the tragic repercussions in the lives of others. Mary is perhaps Eliot's most Chekhovian character. Her routine as under-valued house-companion is broken, and womanly feelings revive in her with the return of Harry. At the end Harry departs and leaves Mary saddened but apparently taking comfort where she can find it. There is in Mary something of Sonia in *Uncle Vanya*, but the pattern of her experience, focused between an arrival and a departure, is similar in outline to that of women in others of Chekhov's plays.

Eliot's appreciation of Chekhov appears to have developed along similar lines to his gradual recognition of poetic qualities in Ibsen. Before hailing Chekhov as his master in 1938, Eliot had tended to link the Russian with the Norwegian as the most acceptable writers within the whole unsatisfactory tradition of superficial realism. These two dramatists 'push realism as far as it can go before it ceases to have artistic form[17].' Even in 1937[18] Eliot appears still to see Chekhov with Shavian spectacles, and not to admire what he sees: at least Chekhov presents profounder problems than Ibsen, even if he does not attempt to solve them. In 1911 Shaw had persuaded the Stage Society to put on *The Cherry Orchard* to introduce Chekhov to English audiences. Defending the play which audiences (including William Archer) had found incomprehensible, Shaw stressed that the play was a social document showing how futile the life of the bourgeoisie could be[19]. Eliot's wording that Chekhov presented 'profounder problems' than Ibsen suggests that for him the Russian remained merely a social realist until just before *The Family Reunion*. However, as early as 1914, in response to a production of *Uncle Vanya*, Desmond MacCarthy[20] had been attempting to assure readers of his review that there was more to Chekhov than this. In 1925 he continued to draw the public's attention to the subtlety of Chekhov's art: 'It is not so much through the literal meaning of remarks, as through the attitudes they betray in the speakers that we are conducted to the heart of the play'. MacCarthy observed that this notion (that the words of characters are pointers to attitudes and feelings that may be implied or given away rather than deliberately expressed) requires careful, minute details in the acting, especially over timing. Chekhov was not at first understood – just as originally he failed in Moscow – because audiences and actors were not used to the style where meaning lay behind the words, not on the surface. Eliot's constant criticism of the theatre during the 1910s and 1920s was that actors were capable of expressing only surface realism, and the thrust of his pioneering a poetic drama was to try to give the theatre material for something more profound. Perhaps Eliot had experience of a poor performance of Chekhov which concealed from him the profounder material in this playwright. It might be a fruitful area of research to trace more precisely Eliot's experience of Chekhov before the Russian, along with Ibsen, leapt into favour shortly before *The Family Reunion* was written. I would suggest that *The Family Reunion* shows that what Eliot recognised as the poetry of these two prose dramatists lies in what we now call the subtext, to which MacCarthy was drawing attention in his reviews. It is, I shall argue, the nature of its subtext which makes *The Family Reunion* a finer play in performance than has often been recognised by literary critics.

The 'subtext' of a play is defined by Stanislavsky, who coined the word and who experimented with a technique for training a new kind of actor partly through the plays of

Chekhov. He calls it 'the inwardly felt expression of a human being in a part, which flows uninterruptedly beneath the words of the text, giving them life and a basis for existing. The subtext is a web of innumerable, varied inner patterns inside a play . . .'[21]. The analysis of the part played by 'recognition' and the confessional duologue put forward respectively by Smidt and Kennedy implies for the actor and actress the existence of such a subtext. The focus of this critical survey now falls on *The Family Reunion* as a text for performance.

Disappointingly, C H Smith's valuable account of the plays in *T S Eliot's Dramatic Theory and Practice* (1963) does not go on to embrace theatrical practice. However, an example of an illuminating combination of literary appreciation with theatrical insight into the play is found in Katharine Worth's discussion of Eliot and the living theatre[22]. She argues that Eliot successfully handled metaphysical questions in a drama of contemporary and human life, and that he pointed in the direction later taken by Pinter and Beckett. She challenges Eliot's own disparaging comments on the play, and wonders if his 'curious judgments' sprang from experience of inadequate productions. She vividly recalls details of Michael Elliott's imaginative production in-the-round in 1966, and shows how the special relationship between actor and audience gave powerful theatrical expression to Harry as both watcher and participant in the events at Wishwood. The Furies were given bold, towering material form under subtle effects of lighting; their ambiguity was conveyed, at first startling the audience at their appearance then, perhaps, seen differently as soaring, upward-pointing beings. The implication is that developments in staging and the design of lighting have released the play from its inhibitions since its earliest productions.

On the human side Katharine Worth notes how characters in the performance moved towards each other as the verse reached its climax in the two 'aria passages'. The 'trance-like, inhuman effect often seen in performance' was avoided. 'The embrace in which they met, sexless, yet touched with sexual tenderness, delicately suggested a real human communion at some deep level of being'. The audience was taken deeper into character, 'communicating below the level of conscious thought'. At the heart of the play, she concludes, is the recognition of ambiguity. This involves the admission that there is 'a neurotic element in the spirituality of Harry and Agatha', and that Amy's 'human criticism of them has validity'. 'As a result the spiritual climax, Harry's private illumination, becomes also a human climax, involving three people, Harry, Agatha and Mary in a delicate emotional consummation which depends for its effectiveness upon an awareness of them as deeply wounded, even crippled, human beings.'

In the pages which follow I wish to suggest that the 'confusion' in our sympathies between mother and son, which Eliot felt to be a flaw, may not be detrimental to the play after all. Rather in performance the play dramatises the tension between various sympathies. The interpretation I am offering may appear to contradict Eliot's original intention when writing the play, but I believe it explains why it is fascinating theatre. Also it suggests that Eliot was a much more perceptive dramatist in his creation of character than either he or many of his critics have realised. The approach taken by critics who have tended to schematise gives us a more or less unified play, but the implication of this unity is that ordinary human beings are seen in a poor light against the hero with his spiritual illumination. At worst, Eliot denigrates human life in favour of divine calling. I wish to question the supposed exclusiveness of Harry's view of the world and the absolute rightness of his behaviour. Once Harry is open to criticism, even perhaps as a prig, the other characters come into their full and significant life. The experience at the centre of the play ceases to be Harry's inner illumination (so difficult in fact to dramatise), and is rather the human consequences on those who are not Harry. There is a tragedy for those who go on living. We are uneasy about Harry's behaviour and final decision because other characters are uneasy. Unlike the Chorus in *Murder in the Cathedral*, who accept the hero's way and are illuminated by it, characters in this play question it or cannot quite cope with it or put a brave face on it. The play is about the difficulty of following a calling; it sees the human consequences even more sharply than the spiritual ones. I shall argue, finally, that the play dramatises tensions deep within Eliot's own experience.

My method of procedure will be to concentrate on the

quality of the characterisation, particularly as revealed in the all-important duologues. I hope to show that the characters are rounded and psychologically coherent. I shall therefore be pointing towards the subtext, through which actors and actresses grow into understanding of the people they are playing. I shall argue that Gaskell's criticism, that actors cannot establish credibility because there is no significant physical action, misses the point: the life and the action, as in Chekhov, lie in the interaction of characters at a level below the surface of the text, and they build to a climax in scenes where the 'taboo on speech' is broken, as in Ibsen. If it can be shown that Eliot is able to create naturalistic characters who offer a challenge to the actors – characters who have their own ways of viewing their life and experience; that Eliot is able to dramatise different concepts of truth and show a dynamic interaction between them; that ordinary people, even if mocked in a comic tradition, have an integrity along with the saints; that the lesser mortals have human emotions and reactions which make their behaviour plausible and sympathetic – if all this can be demonstrated, then it should be possible to counter the claim that Eliot is unable to make the natural world real to our imagination. I suggest that his characters are not representations of attitudes, but people who are created as vulnerable and as capable of growth.

# 2

## Mary

Mary becomes 'one of the most living people in the play, and one of those who has the most hold upon the audience'[1]. This is Martin Browne's observation on the way the character grows through three drafts of *The Family Reunion*. He does not, however, go into detail about the nature of this dramatic appeal. Nevill Coghill[2] also suggests that Mary has a self-effacing, long-suffering side, an 'uncomplaining love' that arouses 'compassion in the audience'. Eliot, however, did not seem to accord her this amount of respect, saying at the time of the second draft of the play that she 'understood nothing' and was an 'evasion' of Harry's spiritual progress[3]. Yet the care he takes in strengthening her characterisation and role in the third draft shows that Eliot the practitioner had imaginative sympathy with the part that as commentator he denied.

Originally Mary was only to 'turn up for' two big scenes (with Harry in Part I and with Agatha in Part II). This plan was a strain on the structure of the play, and it expected too much of the actress to have no preparation for these scenes. In the final version Eliot has given Mary a part in the opening scene which establishes her as an interesting misfit in the family circle, and as a character with a tragic past. The additional lines are from Gerald's 'You're being very hard on the younger generation' (56) to 'That reminds me, Amy,' (79). In this section Mary is given an effective reaction to the out-of-touch comments of the Uncles and Aunts which highlights their patronising attitudes and their ability to wound:

'Really, Cousin Gerald, if you want information
About the younger generation, you must ask someone
                                                else.
I'm afraid that I don't deserve the compliment:
I don't belong to any generation.
                                    *(Exit)*'    (64-7)

The touchiness with which she leaves the room also betrays
that Mary is particularly on edge.

As the additional dialogue continues, two characters reveal
more about Mary's situation. Charles, the uncle who later says
of Harry's crisis that he 'might understand', realises that Mary
is now thirty and unmarried; the Uncles' and Aunts'
comments on her as a member of the younger generation
must have touched a raw nerve if she feels she's on the shelf
(72-4). Amy is able to show her understanding of the situation,
though this is tinged with the bitterness that her own plans for
Harry have gone awry. Mary would have been married

'if things had gone as I intended.
Harry's return does not make things easy for her . . .'
                                                (75-6)

These words reveal a more specific motivation for Mary's
being on edge: Harry and she might have been married, and
his imminent return raises regret for what might have been.
His return is also unsettling because it brings a possibility that
they may be able to take up again where they left off. Amy's
'but life may still go right' (77) shows that she at least has not
let go of her hopes. The dialogue also implies that Mary is a
victim of Amy's personality: she has continued to live under
Amy's roof and on the memories of Amy's thwarted plans for
her.

This inserted section has introduced Mary as a figure of
interest who stands apart and is emotionally volatile: Harry's
return has painful associations which touch upon her lack of
fulfilment as a woman. The scene gives the actress a fine start
for the reunion she has to play later. She is on stage for about
sixty lines, saying nothing but able to get inside the
atmosphere of the play. She is then drawn into the

conversation against her will, and before she leaves the room speaks four lines which just keep control of the pain and bitterness that is rising in her. For the audience, an element of mystery has been created, and the second scene gains in dramatic effect because we are eager to find out what grief lies within this woman.

Mary's next scene was to have begun with a soliloquy[4] which Harry would interrupt, overhearing her last words as he came downstairs dressed for dinner. This soliloquy would have shown Mary uncomfortable in the cold northern climate, worrying about preparation for dinner and then wondering what Harry will be like now. As planned, this would have been Mary's introduction to the audience. Certainly it would have established her as a reluctant housekeeper-companion to Amy, doing the flowers and in charge of the seating plan. But her interest in Harry could not then have had the personal urgency it has already acquired by this stage in the action, so in the final version we are spared a series of awkward rhetorical questions:

'I wonder what Harry is going to be like.
It won't be too easy talking to Harry
After all that's happened. Oh how can I stand it?
Can I stand another season in this house?
What does this place mean? Where everybody
Has always seemed to be waiting, waiting,
Waiting. I think this house *means* to keep us
waiting.'

We are spared this because her nervousness at Harry's return has been so suggestively established in scene one, where it arises naturally through character and situation. Now, in place of a crude use of soliloquy, Eliot continues to unfold character by implication through dialogue.

In the final version, what is left of Mary's soliloquy is transposed into conversation with Agatha, who stays on stage into scene two after the others have left to change for dinner. Indeed, Agatha is assigned some of the lines previously drafted for Mary. Mary begins formally, using the flowers she has brought in as a pretext for talking about the long winters at Wishwood. The hint of regret in the lingering rhythm of spring, 'Late and uncertain, clings to the south wall' (2), develops into a more personal despondency in her next lines on the unnaturalness of greenhouse flowers that do not know the wind and rain as she knows them (5-8). If, through talking about the effect of the late spring on the flowers, Mary is making signs to Agatha that she is depressed by Wishwood and her life there, Agatha does little to encourage her to release the emotions that were already welling up in scene one: 'I always forget how late the spring is, here' (4) is as much Agatha's criticism of Amy's house and its location as it is sharing in Mary's feelings – the wording is hardly warm. Agatha's next one-liner (9) changes the subject as if deliberately holding Mary's more personal remarks   at a distance.

Michael Elliott's Royal Exchange production of the play in 1979 brought out the implications of underlying tension in staging this scene. The direction, *'Enter MARY with flowers'*, was the clue to the action. The hothouse flowers were still in a bunch and needed trimming and arranging in the vase. Mary busied herself in this activity so as to avoid having to look directly at Agatha, and her nervousness was conveyed in the way she worked. Mary started speaking, it seemed, simply to cover the embarrassing silence. Text and performance here enabled the actresses to imply an uneasy relationship between the two women even before some of its history comes into the open. Lines, which followed one another awkwardly in the soliloquy as the train of one person's thought, become dramatically effective instruments for a second person to keep her distance from the working of the other's mind.

Mary is testing the ground for a personal admission, but the 'taboo on speech' is still too strong. The active subtext continues as Mary discusses the dinner arrangements and talks about the artificiality of such

'An official occasion of uncomfortable people
Who meet very seldom, making conversation.' (22-3)

Despite her present awkwardness with Agatha she appears to want the dialogue to go deeper. Her strategy is to

keep up her end of the conversation. She speaks lugubrious-
ly of Arthur and John. Significantly, however, she has hardly
mentioned Harry: with apparent casualness she merely says
that he's arrived (11-12). Yet it is precisely his arrival that is
the cause of all the agitation she has displayed. On the
surface, the agitation takes the form of anxiety about the
seating-plan for dinner. Eliot has provided the actress with
details for hinting in performance at a lively subtext: dare
Mary talk about Harry and her deeper concerns in the
presence of Agatha, her forbidding former college principal?

At last Mary takes the plunge and asks Agatha directly for
advice. Then comes the blast of coldness which the two
women have been holding beneath the surface of their
conversation:

> 'A: I should have thought
>     You had more than you wanted of that, when at
>                                               college.
>  M: I might have known you'd throw that up against me.'
>                                               (29-31)

The nature of a long-standing antagonism becomes
clearer now. There follow three lines crucial to the
appreciation of Eliot's balanced characterisation. Mary has
the strength of character to confront Agatha with the image
she preserves of her from college days:

> 'I only saw you as a hard headmistress
> Who knew the way of dominating timid girls.
> I don't see you any differently now;' (33-5)

As the play goes on the relationship is to improve, but
Mary's unsympathetic judgment of Agatha at this point is
valuable to the audience. In scene one Agatha had come to
be the voice of authority and insight, unquestioned by
anyone except Amy. Now, the former pupil brings to light
the austerity of Agatha which got in the way of her
relationship with students. Some of Agatha's all-seeing
comments on the behaviour of others in scene one are now
brought into perspective. Perhaps Eliot is allowing us to see

faults in Agatha rather than making her the characterless mouthpiece of his own ideas. Alternatively, if we have found her wisdom jarring in scene one, it is perhaps reassuring to find another character within the play casting doubt on Agatha's personal attractiveness. Mary still respects her advice even if she finds the adviser inhumane. This is skilful handling on Eliot's part: Agatha is not denied wisdom, but her kind of insight is bought at a cost in human relationship. The full explanation of Agatha is yet to come in Part II, the hardness of her nature is the result of her own suffering. The tragedy beneath the surface is yet to be revealed, and until then we are allowed to find her less than sympathetic.

Indeed, Agatha acknowledges the force of Mary's critical attitude later in the scene:

'I am very sorry, Mary, I am very sorry for you;
Though you may not think me capable of
                              such a feeling.' (72-3)

She sees that pity may well aggravate Mary in her present state of mind, and she hints that she is not as unemotional as her donnish austerity made her seem. Behind the inter-action of the two characters in this scene is the fact that Mary only knows Agatha from the time after she became a head of college. Mary is not to know that university life was a retreat from the wounded love affair Agatha had with Lord Monchensey. We discover only later the degree to which Agatha's case sympathises with Mary's. The actress playing Agatha in this scene has a subtext on which to draw. She hopes Mary will take the compassionate side of her nature on trust, but she cannot reveal the secrets that would explain her. Mary, however, feels let down; she has not been given the help she wanted. Her opinion of Agatha at the end of the scene is confirmed: 'So you will not help me!' (83).

What, then, makes Mary reveal as much as she does to Agatha during a scene with such underlying mistrust in it? The turning point is the speech beginning, 'Oh, you don't understand!' (41) with its sudden, awkward change to:

'But you do understand. You only want to know
Whether I understand.' (42-3)

Is this *volte-face* just a device to put the audience in the picture and unveil the mystery of her sadness? Or is it a speech justified by character and situation? It is a cold question from Agatha, almost the precision probing of the tutorial, that makes Mary open her heart. Seven years ago, Mary had turned down Agatha's advice to try for a fellowship when Harry left with his wife, yet now she wants Agatha to help her to leave Wishwood. Agatha's 'After seven years?' (41) challenges Mary to face the implications of the timing of her new request for help. At first Mary hears this question as a continuation of hostilities, but then softens her attitude. Agatha's challenge, with its implied, 'Why now?', reaches to Mary's vulnerability in the subtext, and thirty lines later she admits that Harry's return makes it essential she should throw off Amy's tutelage and find a job elsewhere. In performance, the actress would need some help in making the transition from the aggressive, 'Oh, you don't understand!' to the immediately ameliorating, 'But you do . . .'. I have found that some encouraging facial expression or a gesture from Agatha may be needed to give Mary a chance to reassess her response, to have the courage to admit that Agatha's question has probed to the heart of her anxieties. Some such cautious indication from Agatha is consistent with her later claim to be compassionate.

Nonetheless it is interesting that in what follows Mary still protects her love for Harry from the direct gaze of Agatha's authority. She begins by talking about Amy's treatment of her, blaming herself for becoming what she thought Amy wanted her to be: a cheap servant. If Amy could have got her as a daughter-in-law she would also have kept Harry at home. Mary's analysis of Amy hints at her own feelings: 'She only wanted me for Harry ' (51). Here Mary cuts herself short and interjects:

> 'Not such a compliment: she only wanted
> To have a tame daughter-in-law with very little
>                                                     money,
> A housekeeper-companion for her and Harry.' (52-4)

What rankles here is that in her selfishness, Amy never took into account Mary's feelings for Harry. It would have

been something of a compliment had Amy wanted her for
Harry because at least she would have acknowledged there
to be a relationship between Mary and Harry. Mary breaks
off because she reckons that 'She only wanted me for Harry'
is too generous a way of putting it. For a moment real
bitterness, rare in Mary, comes to the surface. The words
'hired servant', 'tame daughter-in-law' and 'she couldn't
bear to let any project go' are charged with resentment.
    Interesting things are revealed, too, when Mary comes to
talk of Harry's wife:

> 'Even when he married, she still held on to me
> Because she couldn't bear to let any project go;
> And even when *she* died: I believed that Cousin
>                                                    Amy –
> I almost believed it – had killed her by willing.
> Doesn't that sound awful?' (55-9)

    In the first line, 'she' still refers to Amy. Although Harry's
wife is not formally introduced into the speech, Mary's mind
runs on and refers to her also as 'she', italicised for some
form of emphasis. What kind of inflection does the actress
put on this word? What attitudes to Harry's wife are
disclosed? Seven years ago, Harry went away with this other
woman and deprived Mary of her hopes, hopes selfishly
encouraged by Amy. What has Mary thought of Harry's wife
all these years? There would seem to be considerable
jealousy behind the use of the pronoun in this way when
logical sentence structure requires the wife to be named
more precisely. The emotional logic does not require such
clarification: to Mary, Harry's wife is 'she' or 'her' – she
cannot be named more personally. Indeed, as Mary has
never met her the woman is hardly real to her. In the
pronoun 'she', all Mary's hurt is implied. Her speech ends
with curiosity: the rejected woman wants to know what the
other was like: 'Did you ever meet her? What was she like?'
(60).
    There is, in the lines (55-9) quoted above, a further point
for the actress. Mary attributes to Amy such jealousy of the
woman who took her son away that she almost willed her
death. We know in this play that Harry's guilt at his wife's

death is because he feels his wish became a reality. Here
Mary detects a kind of victory in Amy when the wife is
drowned. How does a nice girl like Mary come to attribute
such a sinister selfishness to Amy? In seven years might not
such a wish have crossed Mary's mind as well? We do not
know, but the actress approaching the part of Mary has
implied for her in the complexities of the surface text, a rich
subtext on which to build a convincingly rounded
character.

If such an emotional coil is seething beneath the surface
in Mary, it is not surprising that Agatha's rather intellectual
advice finally appears too philosophical to be acceptable.
She tells Mary not to run away from Harry now that he is
coming back: to submit to the will of powers beyond,

> 'You and I, Mary,
> Are only watchers and waiters: not the easiest role.
> I must go and change for dinner.' (81-83)

Mary, in the intensity of her feeling – only barely guessed
in scene one by Amy's 'Harry's return does not make things
easy for her' – senses a rejection in Agatha's words. Once
again, in the lines that follow, what had been unfocused
dramatically in the soliloquy drafted to Mary becomes
forceful in the play. Mary does, finally, speak to herself for
two and a half lines. But this is a kind of outburst prompted
by what she sees as Agatha's continued austerity. 'Waiting,
waiting, always waiting': Mary has picked up Agatha's
words 'waiters', and resents it. As in the draft, Harry enters
on her next line. 'I think this house *means* to keep us
waiting'.

The moment Mary has been dreading has arrived – how
will she fare with Harry after seven years of memories and
desires? The ensuing duologue is shaped to reveal Mary's
sensitivity to Harry moving precariously towards success as
Harry warms to her. Then suddenly, and viciously, he
rejects her.

The sequence begins with Mary suddenly becoming
formal after her tense scene with Agatha. Harry has
overheard her frustrated line – 'I think this house *means* to
keep us waiting – and she pulls back to the safe level of

conversation:

> 'How do you do, Harry.
> You are down very early. I thought you had just
> arrived.
> Did you have a comfortable journey? (86-8).

The security of formality is essential to her in this highly charged reunion. They talk, still very much on the surface, about the way nothing in the house has changed. There is a Chekhovian regret in Mary's comment on their provincial life at Wishwood:

> 'Yes, nothing changes here,
> And we just go on . . . drying up, I suppose,
> Not noticing the change. But to you, I am sure,
> We must seem very altered.' (101-4)

Then comes Harry's first direct attention to Mary beyond the formalities:

> 'You have hardly changed at all –
> And I haven't seen you since you came down from
> Oxford.' (104-5)

Mary immediately looks for an excuse to leave the room. Running away was her resource when embarrassed by the Uncles and Aunts in scene one, and she is to make another attempt to get away later in this scene. So, we may ask, what touches the nerve here? For Mary, so much has changed in her inner life: her prospects of marrying Harry and her fulfilment as a woman have been lost, and she has realised that she has wasted her life in servility to Amy. Harry's comment brings to mind all that might have been. Furthermore the reference to Oxford reminds her of the academic life which she was advised to pursue when Harry left. As we see later in the scene, she is acutely sensitive to the way Harry views her: she fears that to him she is just an intellectual, a bookish bluestocking with no passion and therefore unable to sympathise with him. The fact that he sees no change in her since she came down from Oxford

wounds her on the unspoken level of the subtext. But Harry
will not let her go to change for dinner. She stays and asks what
is, on the surface, a further social question: 'Are you glad to be
at home?' (108). Harry, who in scene one has been unnerving
people by his deep answers to everything, now uses Mary as a
sounding board.

One of the achievements of Eliot's final version of the play
is that he distinguishes between the verse of Harry and of
Mary (see Appendix). Where in an early draft[5] both speakers
were often elevated, almost mystical in their language, here
Harry retains a rhetorical style while Mary is more down to
earth. Harry remains on a philosophical plane, considering
the nature of memories and whether his return to Wishwood
will ease his troubled mind (108-121). He lives life with an
intensity which will not let him relax into pleasantries. Mary,
however, when asked if she was ever happy as a child at
Wishwood, refers more specifically to unhappy experiences of
her childhood.

She also has the courage at this point to turn her
conversation more intimately to Harry, drawing a distinction
between herself and him as children. She concludes:

'We were rather in awe of you –
At least, I was.' (128-9)

The dash is significant: from a general comment she pauses
and risks the personal commitment to what she is saying by
opening up the subject of their relationship. Harry does not
warm to the implication of 'At least I was'. Rather he
continues to use Mary to explore his own reactions to his
upbringing. Reminders come from her of the way everything
seemed planned too carefully to be enjoyed (130ff). Mary even
hints resentment that all seemed to be for Harry's benefit: the
feelings of others were not taken into account. Now, for the
first time, Harry seems to come closer to Mary by including
himself in the awful pattern of the life; he was just as much
manipulated as she felt herself to be (135ff). Then comes the
mutual memory where the two recall the one place of
happiness which they shared as children. The pace of the
dialogue livens up as the sentence is shared between them in
the excitement of recollection:

'H: But do you remember
M: The hollow tree in what we called the wilderness
H: Down by the river. That was the stockade
  From which we fought the Indians, Arthur and
                    John.' (137-40)


It is part of the exultation the characters and audience
experience at this point that the dialogue becomes detailed
and focused in its particulars of the past. The two relive an
authentic experience which brought them close in childhood
and which was sacred because the adults never knew the
importance to them of the hollow tree. The closeness they
share in this memory is then broken because only Harry
knows what happened next: the adults had the tree felled and
removed the wilderness to build 'a neat summer house' to
please the children (150ff). We begin to see why Harry is such a
strange, difficult man. His childhood spontaneity was stifled
by overbearing parents arranging life too neatly for the child's
richer imagination. We begin to appreciate the stunting of
Harry's own emotional life that lies behind his neurotic
behaviour in the play so far.

Once the temporary bonding between Mary and Harry
through their recollection is over, Mary retreats into her adult
anxieties. She leads the conversation from the stupidity of the
older generation to the way her own life at Wishwood is now
unbearable. Then there is a major change in direction: Mary
suddenly cuts off her account of life at Wishwood with an
apologetic:

'But why should I talk about my commonplace
                                   troubles?
They must seem very trivial indeed to you.
It's just ordinary hopelessness.' (162-4)


If it is to be dramatically convincing, arising out of character
and situation, this change of direction on the surface must be
the result of some inner activity of the character. What returns
here is her uncertainty, her awe of Harry, her feeling of
inadequacy, her fear that she will bore him. Perhaps the actor
playing Harry makes some possibly unconscious gesture that
makes Mary suspect that he is not interested in hearing her

problems but wants to talk about his own. Some such indication in the staging to bring about Mary's apologetic tone would be consistent with the mood of his next speech, in which he begins to claim the uniqueness of his own experience: 'One thing you cannot know' (164).

In a rhetorical sequence Harry asserts that her ordinary hopelessness is nothing compared to his kind of hopelessness:

(*) 'One thing you cannot know:
The sudden extinction of every alternative,
The unexpected crash of the iron cataract.' (164-6)

Perhaps Harry has felt that Mary's apologetic tone gave him licence for this slight self-indulgence.

Mary acknowledges that 'the sudden extinction of every alternative' is an experience beyond her, but she will not be fobbed off. She puts it to him that she can understand what he means and suggests that his sense of despair may be an illusion, despite its apparent reality to him. She treads cautiously, for she knows from her own experience with Agatha earlier that advice which misses the intensity of one's feelings is irksome. But she is not totally disinterested. She is trying to awaken Harry to her, to show that she loves him, and she offers him an 'alternative', although he cannot see it. She develops her thought a few lines later:

'That sudden comprehension of the death of hope
Of which you speak, I know you have experienced it,
And I can well imagine how awful it must be.
But in this world another hope keeps springing
In an unexpected place, while we are unconscious of it.'
(183-7)

This is no Agatharian insight nor a generalised perception about hope from another world. It is her way of working round to saying that she is herself that hope. The subtext says, 'I love you'. She is trying to find the language that will get through to Harry in his present state of mind. She acknow-

---

* For defence of Harry's rhetorical intensity see appendix.

ledges the authenticity of his experience and plays down her
own knowledge of hopelessness because she senses that he is
not interested in it. Yet it is because when Harry left she had
herself felt a sudden death of hope that she can sympathise
with what he is going through. Her sympathy is authenticated
by her own experience, and this testifies to the quality of
Eliot's characterisation. Such is her capacity to love that she
plays down how she came by such experience because she
must minister to a mind perturbed. Also she dare not yet risk
explicit statement of her feelings for Harry, such is the taboo
on intimate speech between them at this point.

Harry, however, is wary of being understood and becomes
quite abrupt when Mary pushes her luck by suggesting that
something inside him can be altered:

> 'You do not know,
> You cannot know, you cannot understand' (206-7)

She pleads with him to be more generous to others, urging
him to be patient with those who have 'not had your
experience' (209). She wants Harry to give others a chance and
not claim exclusiveness for his feelings, thereby pushing all
human contact away from himself. But he persists,
'Explaining would only make a worse misunderstanding', a
repetition of the attitude he took in scene one with the rest of
the family until Agatha calmed him down. He now hints for
the first time at the haunting presence of the Furies. Mary
takes umbrage because she is being given no credit, and for
the second time tries to leave:

> 'If you think I am incapable of understanding you –
> But in any case, I must get ready for dinner.' (217-18)

Harry, however, gives her another chance: he senses that
something important is happening – 'Something should have
come of this conversation' (221). Eliot himself has given us
Harry's subtext at such a point as this[6]: he becomes aware of
Mary as a woman for the first time: after the horror of his
marriage he is learning to find a woman attractive. While the
actor can convey this by a softening of his tone and movement
towards Mary physically, such a subtext is not nearly as finely-

tuned to the surface dialogue as is the development of Mary's
loving compassion beneath the constraints on her speech.
Harry's gentler tone encourages her to put her point again.
This time she plays herself down more than ever in what is
perhaps Eliot's most moving piece of writing for the
naturalistic stage. It demands close attention because it is
central to the dramatisation of Mary's tragedy in the play.

> 'I am not a wise person,
> And in the ordinary sense I don't know you very well,
> Although I remember you better than you think,
> And what is the real you. I haven't much experience,
> But I see something now which doesn't come from
> tutors
> Or from books, or from thinking, or from observa-
> tion:
> Something which I did not know I knew.
> Even if, as you say, Wishwood is a cheat,
> Your family a delusion – then it's *all* a delusion,
> Everything you feel – I don't mean what you think,
> But what you feel. You attach yourself to loathing
> As others do to loving: an infatuation
> That's wrong, a good that's misdirected. You deceive
> yourself
> Like the man convinced that he is paralysed
> Or like the man who believes that he is blind
> While he still sees the sunlight. I know that this is true.'
> (222-237)

Mary begins cautiously; she works through the first few
lines to overcome her self-mistrust to offer Harry a diagnosis
of his problems which could misfire – dealing with people at
such a depth where nerves are exposed, as Mary herself well
knows, can be dangerous. The first line is a short one, a pause
intended after, 'I am not a wise person'. This is not false
modesty; she has just held the stage with 'a wise person',
Agatha, and she knows how difficult such people's advice can
be. The inflated style of the first speech drafted for her at this
point[7] has in the final version relaxed into the rhythm of
speech: 'And in the ordinary sense I don't know you very
well'. Her next line, 'Although I remember you better than

you think', has behind it the whole scene with Harry to this point. It was she who helped Harry to evoke detailed memories of their childhood which brought their earlier moment of rapport, but, as we have seen, Harry has indicated several times that he regards his later experiences as unique and beyond anyone else's power to understand. So Mary here acknowledges that he doesn't give her much credit. Then she battles with her hyper-sensitivity to her reputation as an academic. What she is about to say is not seen through the spectacles of books. She is forestalling criticism by urging him not to judge her as the Oxford undergraduate he remembers. Also, for Mary, the academic life held out to her seven years previously represented an escape from the reality of feeling after Harry's departure; an escape into the intellectual and apparently arid world represented by her image of Agatha. Books she associates with the failure of human response, and thus she wants to put these aside:

> 'But I see something now which doesn't come from tutors
> Or from books, or from thinking, or from observation:
> Something which I did not know I knew . . .' (226-8)

She is urging him to take her seriously. Behind the lines, more urgently than before, lies the meaning, 'I love you: I know you think me a scholarly dried old stick, but I am in fact a creature of love and passion; one who, because she has suffered, can understand. Look at me for what I am'. The authenticity of the speech to this point is clear, because her anxiety about the low impression Harry has of her has been justified dramatically in his claims that she cannot understand his unique experience.

The final nine lines of the speech are hard. Continuing in our belief that the speech is authenticated by Mary's subtext, we can interpret as follows. Mary endeavours to suggest to Harry that, just as his experience makes all the promises of Wishwood seem a deception, so his horror at the ensuing nightmare may also be a delusion. She implies that he has got things out of proportion and compares his self-loathing to an infatuation: in a kind of self-indulgence he blinds himself to areas of hope. In her comparison of love to an infatuation – a good that's misdirected – she draws from her own complex feelings. Her hope of marrying Harry was a cheat, and her regretful memories and desires since then have been compounding the felony. Now, as we have seen from her conversation with Agatha, she fears that pursuing her love for Harry would be merely perpetuating her subservience to Amy. She has been trapped by the pattern imposed by Wishwood into feelings which, having no natural resolution, became an infatuation. Harry has apparently never realised that she loved him so strongly, and even if he loved her his rebellion against his mother's programme for his life meant that he had to abandon feelings for Mary. His attitude now suggests that he has gained no greater respect for Mary, and any hopes she may have had of her love reawakening in a positive relationship seem to have been a further delusion. Only if the words of this speech are grounded in her own painful experience of love and disappointment can her final line have authenticity within character and situation: 'I know this is true.' If they are not so based, then the second part of her speech becomes the intrusive voice of Eliot that critics object to, asserting a view whereby human love needs to be channelled to a divine goal, otherwise it is merely infatuation. It may well be that Eliot felt this to be the case, but such a view is not what Mary appears to mean from her standpoint as a character in the human drama of the play.

This time Harry responds positively:

> 'And I hear your voice as in the silence
> Between two storms, one hears the moderate usual
>                                                              noises
> In the grass and leaves, of life persisting,
> Which ordinarily pass unnoticed.
> Perhaps you are right, though I do not know
> How you should know it.' (243-248)

The calmness in Harry's rhythm and imagery here reflects a momentary respite from his mental anguish. The rhetorical flavour of his earlier soul-searching has gone. It provides a psychologically justified lifting of the language to the level of poetry, in preparation for the lyrical duet between himself and

Mary. Despite the grudging generosity of his

> 'I do not know
> How you should know it',

he accepts her capacity for sharing his experience: 'Is the spring not an evil time, that excites us with lying voices'. Both of them have spoken of the deceptive hopes of Wishwood: their sequence of arias signifies the apparent success of Mary's appeal to Harry. As Katharine Worth observed, while they come together in this lyrical passage both physically on stage and in communication below the level of conscious thought, there is still an uncanny mismatch in the focus of their respective use of the images of spring. Mary's language is of the pain of nature stirring for growth. We recall that she preferred the wind-blown flowers of spring to greenhouse ones, for like her they knew the winds and rain. For her, Harry's images of sacrifice and death are transcended in the joy of new life. Harry's images have more sinister overtones, depicting spring as a season of violent sacrifice: it is 'an issue of blood', and he speaks of the wail of the new full tide and images of ghosts and drowning drawn from his experience of his wife's death.

> 'Do not the ghosts of the drowned
> Return to the land in the spring?'

Despite Eliot's belief to the contrary, such lines arise naturally from character in that they express Harry's deepest fear, that the ghost of his drowned wife is haunting him, demanding blood. Both Harry and Mary are true to their feelings below the level of conscious communication in the aria passage, and Harry experiences the temporary release of articulating his fears:

> 'You bring me news
> Of a door that opens at the end of a corridor,
> Sunlight and singing . . .' (283-5)

However, the implications of Harry's vision of spring are to be manifest a few lines later. Instead of being removed from the situation, as Eliot again feared, this aria passage both expresses a joy of communion carefully prepared in the previous scene and, through the different connotations of their respective images of spring, foreshadows the cruel frustration of their rapport with the appearance of the ghosts. Eliot has claimed[8] that the moments of most intense poetry are also the moments of drama in a poetic play: as if in confirmation of this, the image Harry used of hearing Mary's voice as 'in the silence between two storms' precisely sums up the dramatic pattern surrounding the aria passage. There remains the theoretical issue of whether Eliot's recourse to heightened poetic language in a naturalistically conceived play is acceptable or a confusion of styles, and this I shall deal with at a later point.

The Furies slam the door that might have opened into 'sunlight and singing' in Harry's face. He has what is almost a fit, he stares through the window and his speech becomes disjointed. Mary attempts to draw him from the horror, believing at this moment that they are part of his delusion:

'Harry, Harry! It's all *right*, I tell you.
If you will depend on me, it will be all right.'
(312-313)

Then he sees the Eumenides, but Mary claims there is nothing there. From Part II scene iii, it is clear that Mary too has seen the Furies, and therefore, although the script does not make it clear here, she must be pretending not to have seen them to try to calm Harry down. We shall return later to the controversy over Eliot's handling of the Furies. For the moment it is Eliot's dramatising of the relationship between Harry and Mary that concerns us still. Harry turns on Mary in anger and arrogance, insisting finally on the uniqueness of his experience and insulting Mary's sensitivity which Eliot has so carefully enabled her to show during the preceding scene:

'Are you so imperceptive, have you such dull senses
That you could not see them? If I had realised
That you were so obtuse, I would not have listened
To your nonsense. Can't you help me?
You're of no use to me.' (328-332)

If Mary has seen the ghosts the lines are doubly ironic, for Harry is quite wrong in his assessment of her. She has not realised that as far as Harry is concerned she cannot understand him unless she has seen them. She has missed the point of his earlier statement:

'There is only one way for you to understand
And that is by seeing. They are much too clever
To admit you into *our* world.' (213-5)

But there was no way in the dramatic context that Mary could then have known what on earth Harry was talking about. Now in the moment of panic she does not connect and realise the importance of acknowledging to him that she has seen them. Her purpose has been sadly misunderstood. On the other hand, if Mary has not seen them there, Harry's reaction is still unjust. The love she has shown for him deserves some gentler response. He can only react in a violent, insulting outburst that makes his experience more important than anyone else's. She is not dull, obtuse, nor does she speak nonsense. Although at this point Harry is still very confused, he loses the sympathy of the audience more strongly than hitherto. He blames everyone else for not entering into the way he sees things, but he refuses to look into the concept of truth of others because he is convinced of his own uniqueness.

Before leaving this scene it is important to examine Harry's outburst from another angle – the one put by Eliot himself in a letter to Martin Browne during the writing of the play:[9]

'Now, as to Harry's marrying Mary as the right way of ending the "curse" . . . The point of Mary, in relation to Harry, was meant to be this. The effect of his married life upon him was one of such horror as to leave him for the time at least in a state that may be called one of being psychologically partially desexed: or rather, it has given him a horror of women as of unclean creatures. The scene with Mary is meant to bring out, as I am aware it fails to, the conflict inside him between this repulsion for Mary as a woman, and the attraction which the *normal* part of him that is still left, feels towards her personally *for the first time*. This is the first time since his marriage . . . that he has been attracted towards any woman. This attraction glimmers for a moment in his mind, half-consciously as a possible "way of escape"; and the Furies (for the Furies are *divine* instruments, not simple hell-hounds) come in the nick of time to warn him away from this evasion – though at that moment he misunderstands their function . . .'

Mary, Eliot told Browne, 'understands nothing'.

There are several points to be made here. The first is that between the second and third drafts of the play Eliot clearly thought that Harry was right to reject Mary. It is a brutal analysis – one that confirms critics' worst fears about Eliot doing down love of created beings in favour of the divine calling. On the plus side, however, Eliot gives vital clues for the actor trying to grapple with the difficult part of Harry. He explains the subtext in terms of Harry's mental sickness: he is repulsed by women because of his bad experience with his wife. We learn that Harry is attracted to Mary as a person for the first time in this scene, a point of significance in terms of the hopes and the possible development of Mary in relationship with Harry. As I have suggested, this may account for Harry's desire to keep her in the room when she tries to change for dinner. It could also account for the extreme nature of his rejection of Mary. However, his final outburst would need to be accompanied by a strong physical reaction away from her after the proximity of the couple during the arias. This would be confusing because such action would make the Furies responsible for Harry's physical repulsion. However, we are told the repulsion is part of his *sickness,* and the Furies are to cure this illness. The cure entails following them on a  purgatorial path. Moreover, there is nothing elsewhere in the scene, even in the final text, to hint at the subtext of Harry's sick physical repulsion. The actor may manage a certain puritanical distance from Mary early in the scene, but this does not seem inherent in the text in the way that Mary's underlying feelings are conveyed. Thus, helpful though Eliot's comments are, they remain external to the text and the actor has to work hard to integrate them into his performance.

My point is that in Eliot's final rewriting of the scene he brings Mary even more sensitively to life than he did in the second draft. Mary, as we have seen, in fact understands a very great deal. Whatever Eliot may have felt in theory about Harry's divine calling and about his sickness which has to be cured, finally in *writing* the scene he shows an imaginative sympathy with Mary which makes her part a splendid one for an actress. She wins the audience's compassion in such a way that Harry's behaviour, whatever its motivation, is brutal in human terms. What Eliot in fact dramatises here is not a man rejecting the temptation towards human relationship as an evasion from the divine calling, but the human cost of such fanaticism. Harry's sickness can only be cured by the way of purgatory that is peculiar to him. For him it is right but what is right for him is tragically wounding to Mary, and Eliot lets this wounding have full dramatic life on stage.

# Appendix to Chapter 2

An early draft of Part I scene two. is written mainly in an abstract poetic style, very difficult for theatrical presentation[1]. The comments of Mary and Harry are not anchored in situation or character, and their experiences lack detail to focus them for the audience. Mary is often a preacher:

'On the surface there is always the perpetual struggle
With difficult circumstances, unrealised ambitions,
And waking in the morning, the reminder of the ceiling
Of something more for which it is too late.'[2]

Despite the ceiling image, this is vague. In its context in the draft, this speech provokes Harry's first moment of appreciation of Mary – a distant figure he needs to know better:

'I have spent many years in travel,
You have been in England, yet you seem
Like someone who comes from a very long distance
Or the distant waterfall in the forest
Inaccessible, half-heard. Can I ever hear
Or see clearly?'

In the final version this speech of Harry's (238-242) is occasioned by something far more finely tuned to Mary's character: her awe of Harry and her love for him timidly reaching out for help (see above in the section on Mary). In this draft Eliot needed to abandon the echoes of earlier plays. 'The perpetual struggle' takes us back to *The Rock* choruses where, in Eliot's 'second voice'[3] of poetry, the members were speaking for him, 'not uttering words that really represented any supposed character of their own':

> 'However you disguise it, this thing does not change:
> The perpetual struggle of Good and Evil.'[4]

Eliot's new style in *The Family Reunion* demands that speeches have a dramatic motivation in the context of the play. My earlier discussion of the final version of Mary's duologue with Harry shows that Eliot achieved his 'third voice', saying 'not what he would say in his own person, but only what he would say within the limits of one imaginary character addressing another imaginary character'.[5]

There remain, however, objections to Mary's rhetoric in this scene which need to be answered. Again the drafts offer a valuable insight. In the same early draft referred to above, there is one part of the dialogue[6] where Mary drops the mystical tone and criticises Harry for taking himself too seriously. Harry says: 'I need much help,' To this Mary replies:

>                          'No you do not!
> You only need straightforward simple honesty.'

She has just explained him as an actor

> 'Of a single role, fearful of a new one. Because you
>                                     fear
> You may not appear so well in another one.'

Then, when Harry had spoken of his dream-like existence he concluded with these extraordinary expressions:

> 'And the eye adjusts itself to a twilight
> Where the dead stone is seen to be batrachian,
> The aphyllous branch ophidian.'

To this Mary replied:

> '. . . And in a way I think
> You take yourself too seriously, like many people
> Who are highly sensitive.'

This last quotation may not be good writing, but in all these proposed lines for Mary something interesting is going on. At this stage in Eliot's characterisation Harry is a prototype for Edward in *The Cocktail Party* rather than for Celia and the saintly life. Mary comes off her preaching pedestal to try to deflate Harry's egocentricity. In her words we have a hint of Celia, Lavinia and Harcourt-Reilly in the later play attempting to bring Edward down a peg or two:

> 'I see that I've taken you much too seriously,
> And now I can see how absurd you are.'
> > (Lavinia I.3.269-70)

> 'Really, Edward, if you were human
> You would burst out laughing . . .'
> > (I.3.452-3)

> 'EDWARD: I have ceased to believe in my own
> > personality
> REILLY: Oh, dear yes; this is serious. A very common
> > malady.
> > Very prevalent indeed.'
> > (II.116-8)

> 'EDWARD: I must have done a great deal of harm.
> REILLY: Oh, not so much as you would like to think:
> > Only, shall we say, within your modest
> > capacity.'
> > (II.139-41)

It is a measure of the difference between *The Family Reunion* and *The Cocktail Party* that such comments are finely tuned to the comic tone of the latter play and are quite inappropriate to the mood of the former. Thus Mary cannot be allowed in later drafts to undermine Harry in the way she does for a few moments in the examples quoted above. However, in her comments from this early draft cutting Harry down to size there is the suggestion that one part of Eliot recognises that Harry's behaviour is out of proportion.

Whereas Mary is often more relaxed in her speech rhythms by the final version than she had been in much of the early

draft, Harry frequently remains rhetorical. Denis Donoghue[7]
and others have criticised the lines which remain in the
published script:

> 'Where the dead stone is seen to be batrachian,
> The aphyllous branch ophidian.' (180-1)

The criticism is that the Eliotic poetic voice intrudes, taking
over from the character. It may be said, however, that the style
here is inflated because Harry is seeing himself in a dramatic
light. Eliot says[8] that the finest rhetoric in drama occurs in
such situations. Such rhetoric is a clue to character for it shows
us 'from which angle he views himself'. There are instances in
*The Cocktail Party* where Edward also sees himself in a dramatic
light and his language becomes rhetorical. For instance:

> 'Why could I not walk out of my prison?
> What is hell? Hell is oneself . . .' (I.3.416-17)

> 'What devil left the door on the latch
> For these doubts to enter?' (I.3.456-7)

If Edward's inflated language is less tortuous than Harry's it
is because he is less tortured. Whereas it is consonant with the
mood of *The Cocktail Party* that Edward can be quickly deflated,
in *The Family Reunion* Harry cannot.

It is significant that in the earlier draft it was after Harry's
'batrachian' speech that Mary said he took himself too
seriously. The note of criticism suggests that while one part of
Eliot takes Harry seriously, another part knows he is
unacceptably extreme. In the final draft Mary points out that
she thinks Harry is wrong in a way much more subtly
consistent with her character, as we have seen. In getting
Mary's character right Eliot has lessened the explicit questioning of Harry's behaviour. Mary is too in awe of, too in love
with Harry to be able to reply with down-to-earth defusing
comments. Criticism of Harry in the scene, and in the play,
eventually works through Eliot's ability to balance the
audience's sympathy across several characters, rather than
through comic deflation.

# 3

## Agatha and Amy

Eliot delighted in an element of mystery in his play, and critics have pointed out hints of a detective story surrounding the circumstances of Harry's wife's death and the appearance of Sergeant Winchell. But Eliot also creates a more subtle kind of suspense, as we wait to have the inner life of the characters disclosed and the motives for their reactions to one another revealed. We have seen how Mary's edginess in scene one has a poignancy unsuspected by anyone else on stage. Similarly with Agatha – in Part Two, layers of experience are unskinned to make her apparent aloofness comprehensible as her private grief is unfolded to Harry. Then, a scene later, even Amy's unsympathetic dominance is shown to have tragedy behind it. The inner lives of Agatha and Amy are so entwined that it is most revealing to consider in tandem Eliot's disclosure of these two characters.

In the first hundred lines of the play Agatha speaks only one line and is referred to once, yet she is on stage all the time – a strangely disconcerting figure set apart from the chatter of the Uncles and Aunts and the arrangements for the birthday party. These two moments make it clear there is tension between her and Amy.

Agatha's first words, 'Wishwood was always a cold place, Amy.' (13), are more than an informative one-liner. They come from a woman who seldom visits the country mansion and they contain hostility not only to the house but to the lady of it. We learn later that on the one occasion Agatha can remember when it wasn't cold at Wishwood she fell in love with Amy's husband and the seeds of resentment were sown. Agatha's opening line refuses to support Amy in the self-pity of her opening speech; it brings down to earth Amy's heightened language. Nevill Coghill[1] suggests that Amy's lyrical opening shows this forceful character momentarily losing confidence as she ponders her deepest fear – death. We may add that the curtness of Agatha's reply is all the more sharply a refusal to make any compassionate concessions to the elder sister. Although an audience needs a little longer in the theatre to settle down before it can register such nuances, the two actresses are helped in having their tension established this early in the subtext.

The second focus for the tension comes at line 89 when Amy adds a degree of frost to the cold war. After the failure of her opening speech to gain sympathy from any of her brothers and sisters, she jolts them with an uncongenial reminder of mortality – and just before a party too!

'You none of you understand how old you are
And death will come to you as a mild surprise,
A momentary shudder in a vacant room.' (86-8)

This chillingly spare image is evocative enough to discomfort the Uncles and Aunts. Then Amy singles out the strongly silent Agatha:

'Only Agatha seems to discover some meaning in
                                                     death
Which I cannot find.' (89-90)

On one level Eliot might seem to be preparing Agatha as the person with special insight who will direct the audience to the play's true meaning; this is how it seems to those who would schematise the play. However, there is more drama here than thematic signposting. Amy's words are resentful. Since Agatha has said nothing about death Amy must be interpreting her enigmatic silence in the light of past experience. Perhaps she wishes she had something of Agatha's apparent sense of purpose: there is an element of lament in the old woman contemplating the loneliness of death. But her regret at not having Agatha's elusive comfort is expressed in terms of envy, and the envy is in turn a kind of mockery. Having unsettled their sisters and brothers-in-law with the momentary shudder in the vacant room, Amy now tries to make Agatha uncomfortable in front of the family for having something they all lack. If Agatha does have some unique vision, Amy resents it as a kind of moral superiority. It is this antagonism that Eliot dramatises.

The deliberateness with which Amy has soured the atmosphere here is apparent from the gratuitousness of the comments. Gerald had asked, 'When are the boys all due to arrive?' (80). Amy delays her reply by ten lines until she has unsettled everyone with her talk of death and her jibe at Agatha: 'I am only certain of Arthur and John . . .' (91).

The conversation then comes to Harry. Previously, as we have seen, he was mentioned in relation to Mary in Eliot's crucially inserted dialogue (56-79). Now we hear of Harry's return in the context of Amy's birthday party: it is to be a special occasion, the first time the whole family has been together since Harry went away. It is now that Agatha speaks at length for the first time. It is over Harry that the implicit tension between the two women is developed, indicating to the audience the field on which their battle is fought. When Agatha speaks of Harry's return, she is the first to consider the home-coming from Harry's point of view rather than the family's self-absorption:

'It is going to be rather painful for Harry
After eight years and all that has happened
To come back to Wishwood.' (107-9)

In this first, albeit oblique, reference to Harry's unhappiness, Agatha becomes a more sympathetic figure. Her point is that Harry will discover how much he has changed since he left Wishwood, even though Amy has kept things as much the same as possible (111-135). The house dominates the play in that, in its very unchangedness, it will provide the contrast by which Harry can become aware of his own movement. At first Amy does not catch Agatha's meaning about Harry finding a new Wishwood: 'Nothing is changed, Agatha, at Wishwood' (121). Amy frequently uses people's Christian names in her speeches – it is part of her control over people – but only here does the name pointedly interrupt the flow of the sentence, highlighting the name like a warning. Eliot anchors Amy's antagonism in a detail of the verse.

Agatha's speeches in sympathy with Harry are complex. The audience senses something of the cryptic nature of Agatha that so infuriates Amy. There is, for instance, her donnish witticism referring to Henry James's short story, *The Jolly Corner*, in which another man returns to a house to search for the person he might have been had he not left home (133). We are perhaps grateful to Gerald for his nice piece of comic placing after her elusive talk of 'the loop in time . . .':

> 'I don't in the least know what you're talking about.
> You seem to be wanting to give us all the hump.'
> (136-7)

Agatha's heightened language is now balanced by forthright colloquialism and by incomprehension.

Gerald's response is not simply foolishness. Agatha and Amy do not make sense to the Uncles and Aunts because their conversation is born of an ancient grudge – not out in the open – between the two sisters. It is too simple a view of Eliot's dramatic writing to argue that the Uncles and Aunts are obtuse in not understanding the prophetic voice of Eliot in Agatha. Their incomprehension is dramatically focused in the fact that they do not understand the battle going on between Agatha and Amy through these speeches. It will be a part of my later argument about the balance of Eliot's characterisation that the Uncles and Aunts, far from being obtuse, are being deliberately manipulated by Amy into a situation where, with the best will in the world, they can only appear stupid. Indeed, immediately here Amy uses Gerald's remarks to her own ends. She approves Gerald's hope that Harry will marry again and settle at Wishwood:

> 'Thank you, Gerald. Though Agatha means
> As a rule, a good deal more than she cares to betray,
> I am bound to say that I agree with you.' (143-5)

While appearing to appreciate Gerald, Amy snipes at Agatha in the choice of phrase,'more than she cares to betray.'

Amy recognises and resents Agatha's cultivated enigma.

Their scene together in Part II brings this out fully, but here it is appropriate that the first stage in the development of the tension is over Harry. For Amy, Harry's return is part of her plan to control the future of Wishwood, with marriage – to Mary perhaps – still part of the scheme. For Agatha, the concern is about Harry himself, and appears to be the less selfish. However, when the dénouement comes we recognise that the tension between the two women is a rivalry over Harry himself, and that this rivalry is a continuation of rivalry over Amy's husband. Ibsenesque secrets lurk in the past of these two characters.

When Harry enters, the different attitudes of the women are enacted in their responses. Amidst all Harry's strange behaviour, his rudeness, even apparent lunacy, Amy keeps up the formal code of conduct: servants have jobs to do and respects to pay to the master of the house. Harry's eccentricity is put down to tiredness, the need of a good night's rest to adjust to country life. A bath will do him good, a servant, of course, turning the taps. Agatha, on the other hand, does not try to behave as if nothing has happened. She encourages Harry to thrash out his confused ideas even though they hit the family like a bombshell. Such ostentatious sympathy for Harry's disturbed state of mind, flying in the face of Amy's express command to the relatives, must fuel the fire of her resentment further. Thus while Harry speaks his complicated speeches, the tension between Agatha and Amy is active beneath the surface. We shall return to the content of Harry's dialogue later.

It is not until after Harry has left to change for dinner that Amy's abrasiveness towards Agatha is heard again. The Uncles and Aunts enter the debate previously wrestled out between Agatha and Amy. Clearly Harry needs calming down; the question is what method will touch him. They want to consult Dr Warburton. Amy prefers to believe that the family atmosphere will have a healing effect – ironic when the family is fraught with unspoken tensions, to be further uncovered when we discuss the Uncles and Aunts. However, Amy agrees to the possibility of bringing Warburton in, provided she is the one to speak to him. Then, pointedly, she asks: 'What does Agatha think?' (418). Given all that has gone before, this cannot be a genuine wish to consult Agatha's opinions. Rather, Amy again exposes Agatha's supposed superiority to public assessment, but she is also curious to know what this enigmatic, dangerous person does think about Harry's problems. Coldly perhaps, but shrewdly, Agatha sees that the doctor must be called to salve the conscience of the family: they will feel they've done the right thing even though it falls short of what Agatha thinks is necessary. Amy, knowing full well that Agatha means more than 'she cares to betray', ignores the implied criticism of the family's embarrassment at Harry's behaviour; she responds practically, taking Agatha's comments as approval for her action. Thus Amy demystifies Agatha's oracular reply by treating it in a business-like manner.

Both Agatha and Amy think it is pointless to consult the doctor, Agatha because she knows that Harry's cure can only come through deeper understanding of his situation, Amy because she thinks he'll come round in the morning. Agatha allows for change; Amy does not. Despite the oracular aloofness of her style, Agatha has attempted to communicate with Harry's immediate feelings. She goes out to him in a way no one else does until his meeting with Mary in scene two.

We have seen from her conversation with Mary (I ii) that Agatha claims she is more capable of human feelings than she revealed as principal of a women's college. However, it is not until her duologue with Harry that Eliot reveals the experiences which lie behind her apparent aloofness. I shall leave detailed discussion of Part II scene ii for the later section on Harry. As my immediate aim is to follow the relationship of Agatha and Amy, I will simply use this scene to draw out the information about Agatha that we take with us into her final confrontation with Amy.

A major revelation comes at the lines following 78. Agatha, having made no sympathetic concessions to Amy in Part I, shows that she is not, after all, insensitive to Amy's feelings. Answering Harry's questions, Agatha explains something of the secret of his parents' lives. Her lines prepare for her confession of near-adultery with Harry's father:

'You see your mother as identified with this house –
It was not always so. There were many years
Before she succeeded in making terms with Wishwood

Until she took your father's place, and reached the point
                                                    where
Wishwood supported her, and she supported Wish-
                                                    wood.
At first it was a vacancy. A man and a woman
Married, alone in a lonely country house together,
For three years childless, learning the meaning
Of loneliness.' (78-86)

There is much of importance here for a production of the
play. The lines are a clue to the set designer, who needs to give
substance to the bleakness of the place – to reinforce through
scenic metaphor the reported experience of Amy.[2] The lines
also give the actress studying the part of Amy insight into the
early years of her marriage and the bitterness these gave rise to
and which she lives out in the play. For Agatha, the lines are
vital in revealing her understanding of Amy's unhappiness,
the difficulty Amy had in coming to terms with living in the
lonely house cut off from family and friends, and then the
horror of the marriage itself, which became the estrangement
of two people under that one roof. The speech is crucial to our
understanding of the tragedy in the relationship between
herself and Amy: Agatha can speak compassionately about
Amy's unhappiness here to Harry, but never can she speak
thus to Amy herself.

Agatha has her knowledge of Amy's loneliness because she
had been her companion at Wishwood in the third year of the
marriage. She was the sister to be invited because she was the
youngest (86-7). Even if she resented such a duty, this speech
shows she might have been able to remain objective about
Amy's sadness had not the 'summer day of unusual heat'
roused her passions. For Agatha, the sudden love between
herself and Amy's husband cried out for, even if it did not
achieve, physical union. This was the one moment of sexual
awakening in her life, and with the eventual frustration of her
love her womanhood remained unfulfilled. Agatha's language when she speaks of saving Amy from the murderous plans
of Lord Monchensey has a maternal and physical urgency,
identifying the unborn Harry in Amy's womb as the child she
herself desired to bear and mother:

'If that had happened, I knew I should have carried
Death in life, death through lifetime, death in my
                                                womb.
I felt that you were in some way mine!
And that in any case I should have no other child.'

(115-18)

It is as if she resents Amy for having given birth out of an
unhappy marriage to the child she might have conceived in
ecstasy.

Agatha has suffered in silence the intense private grief of
this illicit affair. In the silence she elected a spinsterhood
which led to austerity; she trained herself out of the need for
human love, a hard-won 'dispossession' (52). As principal of a
women's college in her subsequent life, she has eschewed the
company of men, living among women, trying – as she puts it
to Amy later – not to dislike women. We have seen how one of
her students, Mary, found her aloof. Now that we see the grief
that led to this coolness we can appreciate something of the
pain she must have felt when Mary criticised her in I ii: a
woman whose capacity for passion forced her into austerity
must find cruel the irony of being judged incapable of
compassion.

Agatha is no saint. She is forced into spiritual consolation
because of the pain she has been given by human experience.
Her insights into this scene as Harry's guide are not neatly
schematised by Eliot to reveal spiritual truths hidden from the
other characters: they are hard-won and costly to this
character. The drama is on the human level: in order to speak
about Harry's father and help him to understand that he is the
child of a loveless marriage, she is also breaking down years of
carefully constructed protective silence in her own life.

The nature of the drama and characterisation which we
have merely asserted here will be demonstrated in detail in the
section placing II ii in the context of Harry's progress in the
play. For our present investigation into the mystery of Agatha
and Amy's hostilities, this scene has been important for
breaking the 'taboo on speech' about Agatha's past, and for
leading into the final encounter between the two women. The
tremors of their conflict, which we saw disrupting the surface
text of Part I, are caused by the continued energy of these

emotions from the past experience and rivalry of the sisters. When Harry announces his departure, the true nature of the women's resentment of each other forces its way to the surface.

Having seen into Agatha's painful life we now see into Amy's tragedy. In scene iii the actress can now make explicit the older sister's suffering that has so far remained hidden beneath dominance and crabbiness. The sympathies balance out again – we have our assessment of Agatha's suffering put into new perspective in the light of the pain she causes Amy.

The confrontation between Amy and Agatha must rank among Eliot's finest dramatic writing. The dialogue is charged with years of resentment. The lines, like Racinian couplets, just hold in check emotion straining at the leash to savage the other, reopening wounds that never healed beneath the surface. So far, with Harry and Agatha, Amy has tried to behave as if nothing has happened – neither Harry's unhappy marriage, nor Agatha's affair with Lord Monchensey. But once she overhears Agatha saying to Harry, 'You must go' (II ii 281), the first layer of formality and dutiful behaviour is stripped from Amy's wound. Despite Harry's protest that Agatha has nothing to do with his decision to depart (II ii 287ff). Amy's most powerful inner resentment dominates against reason. For her, Agatha's possessive instincts are at work again, thirty years on. At this stage she challenges Agatha with: 'He shall go? And who are you to say he shall go?' (II ii 284). Behind these lines lies Amy's resentment of Agatha, the rival for her husband's affections and the intruder now on her plans to make Harry master of Wishwood. Agatha is seen to be undermining Amy's whole purpose in life.

In scene iii, when the two women are alone, the relationship is stripped to its core:

> 'Thirty-five years ago
> You took my husband from me. Now you take my son.'
> (4-5)

From Amy's perspective, Agatha was to blame in taking her husband, and her husband was weak to be misled by an unscrupulous woman (75-6); now Agatha is repeating her rapacity.

In defence, Agatha replies that Amy's marriage had already broken down before Agatha even came to Wishwood; indeed, as we have seen, Agatha was invited to alleviate Amy's loneliness. The rhythm of Agatha's speech rises to the occasion. No longer does she speak in her oracular style, but bitingly, staccato and bitter. The repetitive pattern of the lines just holds the feelings in check:

> 'What did I take? Nothing that you ever had.
> What did I get? Thirty years of solitude . . .' (6-7)

Agatha then expresses her private grief. She no longer uses the ascetic terms in which she revealed it to Harry as hard-won 'dispossession' and a life-time's march across 'a whole Tibet of broken stones'. Instead, we have a rueful repetition of the word 'women' to emphasise the pain of her life cloistered from fulfilment with men:

> 'Alone, among women, in a women's college,
> Trying not to dislike women.' (8-9)

Then her 'Do you suppose that I wanted to return to Wishwood?' (10) fires out from the personal bitterness in delayed reply to Amy's 'I was a fool, to ask you again to Wishwood;' (1).

Eliot's empathy with the two women in this scene is evidenced in such details whereby they do not immediately reply to the points raised by the other, but come to them through the bursting of the dam which holds back thirty-five years of frustration with each other. Thus Amy does not respond immediately to Agatha's bitter account of her life ruined by the affair with Lord Monchensey. While Agatha was speaking, Amy had been digesting the implication of Agatha's opening question, 'What did I take?' This question challenged Amy to admit that her marriage was miserable before Agatha joined her during that hot summer, and therefore that Agatha cannot be to blame from breaking up something Amy never had. It is a harsh confession from Agatha, showing no sign of remorse. It is not even a case of being cruel to be kind; this is no Agatha of spiritual superiority, but a woman speaking from deep within her own tragic life.

Amy begins her next speech by conceding Agatha's point and going on to expose what she sees as Agatha's even greater heartlessness:

> 'The more rapacious, to take what I never had;
> The more unpardonable, to taunt me with not having it.'
> (11-12)

'Rapacious' and 'taunt' are rapier words that pierce years of control each woman has built round herself. The lines still maintain an ordered balance of phrases whereby the pressure of the inner loathing to find expression is intensified. We are now approaching the heart of the antagonism from Amy's point of view: Agatha's affair with Lord Monchensey exposed the hollowness of the marriage and Amy saw this as a sister's mockery of her misfortune. Harry's departure now is a further devastation of the same kind.

Amy, like Agatha, has had her life frustrated; her urge to creativity has gone sour. The lines that sum up her tragedy are:

> 'What of the humiliation,
> Of the chilly pretences in the silent bedroom,
> Forcing sons upon an unwilling father?' (19-21)

These lines give a greater personal depth to her image in Part I of death as a momentary shudder in a vacant room – death for her is described in the terms she understands: loneliness and chilly rooms in a bleak, hostile house. In these lines she reveals that her will to have children had become soured into a desire to shame her husband for his disloyalty by producing two more sons (Arthur and John) to be substitutes. Her marriage having no ecstasy, she clings to the future to give purpose to her life. She saw it as a moment of weakness to let her husband leave her, but she makes up for it by forcing herself 'to the purposes of Wishwood' (26). In her wishes for Harry, what might have been creative became possessive and stifling, but she does not yet recognise this. Her aim became the perpetuation of the family at a house she never liked in the first place – such is the irony of a soured life. Her way of life now depends on formality and duty to support it; the admission of failure is forced beneath a protective clothing that makes Amy able to go on living – but partly living – just as Agatha found her security in the austerity of a women's college. The two sisters have much in common, as Agatha is later to point out (52-4).

Part of the protective defence – behaving as if nothing had happened – led to Amy inviting Agatha back for visits after Lord Monchensey was gone: 'So that there might be no ugly rumours' (28). For a moment there is an air of triumph in Amy as she declares, 'You thought I did not know!' In such an atmosphere, even if Agatha wanted to be reconciled to Amy it is impossible for her to show her mercy: here the love Agatha felt for Lord Monchensey, which was her one moment of sexual awakening, is reduced by Amy to the level of a sordid affair. In a way, both women are right; Eliot's delicacy is in seeing both women's concept of truth, and dramatising the resultant conflict. Furthermore, if Agatha loved the man she must resent the bitterness with which Amy speaks of his weakness: 'You may be close, but I always saw through *him*.'

Agatha replies from the heart, and we can recognise from Amy's behaviour in the play the truth in what she says:

> 'But you are just the same:
> Just as voracious for what you cannot have
> Because you repel it.' (35-7)

'Voracious' here fights back against Amy's earlier 'rapacious', and this time Agatha hits home to the tragic heart of Amy. She sees that Amy's character is such that she puts off the very people that she has most need of. This is an interesting speech of Agatha's for it is not oracular in its truth-telling. Her tone is softened by a moment of inner reflection where she becomes humble about her own ability to change (32-5). Earlier, with Harry, she had spoken of being tired, as the old are, at the beginning of an action, and she regretted that she had lived on spiritual capital rather than earning her income daily (II ii 149ff): she acknowledged that austerity had put a freeze on her growth. Now with Amy she is saying that at last she is trying to change; her irritation is that her elder sister persists in the falsehood she has built around her in self-preservation.

Amy's reply confirms that she is still living the protective lie. She refers to Harry being a happy boy at Wishwood, but we know that Harry resented the adults stifling his childlike imagination by arranging things the grown-up way. Agatha then appears to adopt her sibylline tone to define success as 'what we can make of the mess we have made of things'. These words are humanised, however, by the experience which lies behind them: Agatha has made a mess of things, and her hope is that the ascetic life she has imposed on herself will bring her to a final joy (II ii 93ff). Thus she has put her faith in a relative kind of success still to come at the end of her painful acceptance of tragedy. This private history behind the words makes more authentic her urging Amy to accept Harry's choice as such another relative success after his own messed-up marriage and the loveless mess into which he was born.

However, Amy knows how to sting with her tongue. With an instinct for Agatha's vulnerability she now throws in her face the lines she did not appear to have heard where Agatha spoke of her ascetic life amongst women (8-9):

> 'Your fury for possession
> Is only the stronger for all these years of abstinence:'
> (48-9)

Agatha's 'dispossession' is now twisted by Amy into a monster's fast, making her all the hungrier for prey. She tries to undermine Agatha's faith in her relative success by seeing it as failure, and by defending Harry from its influence.

Agatha now tries to defuse the situation, but her attempt to equate their two experiences serves only to antagonise Amy further:

> 'Why should we quarrel for what neither can have?
> If neither has ever had a husband or a son
> We have no ground for argument.' (52-4)

This is perhaps the closest Agatha comes to a sympathetic

comment, showing that she recognises Amy's inner sense of failure as wife and mother; she urges reconciliation on the grounds of common unhappiness in unfulfilled womanhood rather than on the false terms designed by Amy at lines 37-44. The hurt in Amy is too deep: she cannot take such words from the woman she sees as her rival rather than companion in suffering. And perhaps she is right – after all, Agatha, while speaking literally of herself, can only speak metaphorically of Amy, who was in fact married and bore sons. Unable to accept Agatha's interpretation of her life, Amy challenges her: 'Who set you up to judge?' (55).

This is the crucial question. If we see the play as a hierarchy of spiritual characters, with Agatha higher on the scale than Amy, the question shows Amy's spiritual blindness in Eliot's scheme of things. On the other hand, if we allow the artistic creation of characters who develop independent lives to take precedence in our reading of the play, the question arises directly out of their conflict. Indeed, who did set Agatha up to judge? She has been cold to Amy from her first line in the play, she has irritated her with cryptic comments in Part I, and she has all but committed adultery with her husband. Far from thinking how obtuse Amy is at this point, the audience feels a sharper tension: if only Agatha could communicate to Amy all that she managed to impart to Harry; if only Amy's tragedy did not harden her against Agatha's; if only Agatha's did not harden her against a more gentle approach to Amy. The answer to Amy's question would be that Agatha's own experience and her way of coping with it qualifies her to minister to Harry and even risk an overture to Amy. She is a wounded surgeon, in so far as she is a surgeon at all in the play.

At Amy's death, the two remain unreconciled, lonely, unfulfilled women. The major difference is that Agatha, having been invited to Wishwood and having chosen for herself the penance of the women's college, understands more of Amy than she lets Amy understand her. Amy's view of Agatha is not to change now. When Mary enters (68), Agatha is 'That woman there' (72), and 'any unscrupulous woman' (76), and when the Uncles and Aunts return their questions are met by the iteration of 'Ask Agatha' – words endowed by Eliot with thirty-five years history perpetuated now in a refusal to compromise to any degree with the younger sister. Coghill[3] has suggested that Amy shows some indication of insight when she replies to Violet, 'Harry is going away – to become a missionary'. If so, it is indeed an 'astounding leap of intuition'. It is based, however, on what Harry has half-hinted earlier (II ii 331ff), rather than on anything Agatha has said. Indeed her line may even be taken as some kind of sneer at Agatha's expense, as suggested by D E Jones (p.106).[4] This, together with Amy's final speech of the play, where she admits to having wanted too much of her children, will be further examined when we look at Harry and Amy.

The outcome of Amy's duologue with Agatha is that she sees her life's purpose in ruins. Mary, her companion, is also about to leave, turning to Agatha for advice on a fellowship, and Amy is to be left alone. Again Agatha is seen as the destroyer. Amy recognises, perhaps in a self-dramatising light, that her purpose has dissolved, and appropriately she links this through images to the destruction of the house (123ff):

> 'So you will all leave me!
> An old woman alone in a damned house.
> I will let the walls crumble. Why should I worry
> To keep the tiles on the roof, combat the endless
> weather,
> Resist the wind?'

The house that she hated at first, but then became identified with, she now leaves to rack and ruin – an admission that her plans have failed. It is a speech of bitterness, not one of insight into her false strategies of self-preservation. It is aimed at making Agatha and Mary feel guilty for destroying her in this way, and thus it is a gesture consistent with her lie; it is not a release from it.

# 4

## The Uncles and Aunts

The Uncles and Aunts have been called obtuse[1]. Schematisers of the play imply that Eliot makes them lesser mortals deliberately, to expose the lowest people in the spiritual hierarchy and ridicule their blindness. The Uncles and Aunts are also out of favour because they speak both as individuals and as chorus in a confusing mixture of naturalism and ritual. Further, they tend to be lumped together as if each uncle and aunt has no personal dramatic contribution to make to the play; even as sympathetic a commentator as Nevill Coghill[2] says that Violet is barely distinguishable from Ivy – not an encouraging analysis for the actresses trying to identify the characteristics of their parts. What Coghill and others apparently fail to see is that through the Uncles and Aunts Eliot dramatises the existing tensions within the family, quite apart from the particular crisis occasioned by Harry's return. They are vital to the play's sense of family, but of a family sharply divided because of the different lifestyles and experiences of its members. The behaviour of the Uncles and Aunts shows that Amy's attempt to hold a family reunion is essentially absurd, since no unity is there in the first place.

Furthermore, the comedy in their presentation has a more dramatic relation to the main action than to give the spiritual journey of Harry dignity in contrast to the farcical misunderstandings of supposedly stupid relatives. Certainly there is comedy, in that we recognise aspects of the theatrical country-house types. But this is not the whole story. They are funny because we can recognise the authenticity of the frustrations which are portrayed between members of a family. Eliot has observed real life as well as country-house comedies. But the effect of the comedy is more subtle yet. The characters of the Uncles and Aunts are clearly amusing, although they do not realise it. Yet they also reveal that they dread being laughed at. The irony of their position is that Amy does perceive their absurdities and makes capital out of them. It is because she helps to make them laughable that we come to sympathise with their dilemma and question our own laughter at them. Because we are drawn into sympathy with their predicament whereby other characters in the play place them at social and emotional disadvantage, their reactions enable us to review and criticise the behaviour of the main protagonists. Thus we have a much more rounded and balanced play than schematisation allows.

While it is the choric passages that release the deeper fears of the Uncles and Aunts, we can go a long way in understanding them just from their more naturalistic conversation. By highlighting first what are in fact crucial differences between Ivy and Violet, we can see something of the disunity in the family gathered for reunion. We should remember, also, that the Uncles and Aunts represent the two families that came together only because Amy married Lord Monchensey. The ties between Ivy and Violet on the one side and Gerald and Charles on the other have no cause to be strong, least of all since the marriage has since broken down. As well as the interfamilial tension between the Monchensey men and Amy's sisters, to which we shall return, there is little family harmony even between the sisters.

Ivy lives in straightened circumstances. Her comparative lack of money has become something of an obsession with her, particularly while staying with her dowager sister at Wishwood. Ivy used to live in Cornwall, where she kept a garden (I iii 10). In talking to Mary she inserts the telling half-line: 'When I could afford a garden', thus drawing attention to her concern about money. Now she lives in a cold apartment in Bayswater – the unfashionable side of Hyde Park and, between the wars, declining in prosperity. She focuses in her opening speech on her need to count the shillings as she sits by the metered gas-fire (I i 18). When Amy dies, Ivy becomes concerned about whether her return ticket to London will still be valid if she stays on for the funeral as she ought (II iii 313). This is not as stupidly trivial in the face of a death in the family as it might seem: she cannot afford a further ticket for the single fare. Finance seems to be at the root of her resentment of Amy, and it is appropriate that concern about the train fare is her distraction from facing the grief of her elder sister's sudden death. At the start of the play her advice to Amy to go south in the winter has a sting in it, for Ivy says she would go south herself but she cannot afford to, whereas, it is implied, Amy can:

> 'I would follow the sun, not wait for the sun to come
> here.
> I would go south in winter, if I could afford it . . .'
> (16-17)

She then tries to shame Amy with her image of feeding the gas meter to keep warm.

Ivy's narrow horizons are not part of a neat spiritual scheme imposed by Eliot. She has had a tougher lot socially than Amy, who is the only one of the four sisters to marry, let alone marry into wealth. Ivy has to support herself, presumably on her inheritance from her parents and, for her as for many spinsters of her generation, this did not stretch far. Hearing Amy complain about Wishwood naturally provokes Ivy's sense of righteous self-pity. She does not understand the associations that make Wishwood such a miserable home for Amy; to Ivy, the house represents the success she never had.

However, Ivy has family loyalty. She visits Cousin Lily in Sidmouth – indeed, prefers her company to Amy's. She recalls with some affection John and Arthur as small boys (II i 297-302), and has a rapport with Arthur such that it is she whom he rings when he's made a fool of himself crashing his car. Ivy's one hobby was gardening, and being now cooped up in Bayswater she is deprived of her horticultural creativity for which she won prizes in Cornwall. This accounts for her being unable to resist tampering with Mary's flower arrangement (I iii 7). Mary is hurt by this interference, especially as her arrangement was done under considerable stress, as we have seen. Ivy's blindness in being insensitive here can be understood given her frustrated creativity. A difference between Ivy on the one hand and Agatha and Amy on the other in their respective frustrations is that Ivy manages to infiltrate her grouses into the conversation; Amy and Agatha have built a taboo on speech around theirs.

Ivy is not, however, unintelligent. She is interested in medicine and encourages Dr Warburton to speak about his 'very rich experience' in forty years as a doctor (I iii 58). From listening to others she has also picked up insights into psychiatry (I i 396) which enable her to make a comment on Harry's behaviour which, as we shall see, is not as irrelevant as the spiritual schematisers would have us believe.

While Ivy's tension is primarily with Amy, Violet sides with the dowager but snipes liberally at others, particularly Agatha. She seems to have kept up with the socially superior more successfully than Ivy, helping Lady Bumpus (I i 210), and she seems to think it important to have the respect of the vicar (I i 210, II iii 163). As Charles points out, ruefully licking his wounds, Violet is worried about her status as Amy's sister (I i 577). Violet sides with Amy in disapproving of Harry's late wife and, taking her cue from Amy's 'blessed relief', Violet calls the wife's death 'providential' (I i 154). She supports Amy's request that when Harry returns they all behave as if nothing has happened, despite Gerald's protest that this is a tall order (188). When Charles suggests speaking to Downing, one reason for Violet's dissent is that she is sure Amy would disapprove of it ( I i 446). When Harry ridicules John after his accident, Violet aims to score points with Amy by urging Harry to show some consideration for his mother's feelings (II i 261). At Amy's death Violet's concern, balancing Ivy's worry about her return ticket, is to wait at Wishwood until the will has been read: perhaps some money from Amy might make it easier for her to sustain her social pretensions.

Violet is obviously snobbish in her comments on those whose wealth is from commerce rather than inherited (I i 41), and she despises travel abroad because she abhors the vulgar company of English holidaymakers. Her exchanges with Ivy suggest that Violet feels superior to her socially, rejecting her suggestion that Amy should go south in winter 'to the military widows and the English chaplains' (I i 20). She makes a jibe at Ivy's rapport with Arthur: 'When it's Ivy that he's asking for, I expect the worst' (II i 348). She likes only the right kind of attention: newspaper reports and lolling back in Arthur's sporty car make one unwelcomely conspicuous to the populace! She disapproves of consulting the servants (I i 566). Her contempt for Harry's choice of wife is conveyed in the slur on her character implied in her question: 'Had she been drinking?' (I i 160) the night she died. However her question misfires for Amy responds with a certain moral rectitude: 'I would never ask him'. Violet has broken a taboo by even mentioning the possibility of Harry's wife taking to alcohol, even though we are to learn from Downing's delicately worded speech that her Ladyship 'wasn't one of those that are *designed* for drinking', as he implies that she over-indulged in cocktails in the evening (I i 504). Amy's final assessment of Violet is that she is the most malicious of the relatives 'in a harmless way' (II iii 192).

It is Agatha's moral tone that particularly sets Violet's teeth on edge and she several times makes her dislike of Agatha public (II i 281, 355, 403-4). Perhaps she senses that Amy also finds her irksome. Also, Agatha is the only one of the sisters to have had a university education and to have earned her own income, through teaching. Intellectually and financially Agatha stands apart from the family, and again one suspects that Violet finds this hard to take. Although Violet credits Ivy with little capacity for understanding things (II iii 262-4), Violet is the one who actually takes the least intelligent interest in life.

It is also Violet who stirs up most of the inter-familial friction with the Monchensey brothers. We have already seen how she closes the sisterly ranks when Amy's wishes are threatened. Ivy associated herself with Violet in disapproving of Charles's decision to interview Downing (I i 455-56). Agatha, fuelling Violet's suspicion of her, dissociates herself from her sisters: she does not object to consulting Downing because she sees it as irrelevant anyway, and leaves the room. The comedy is that Ivy and Violet nonetheless stay to witness the dialogue of which they disapprove because they do not wish to be left out, and presumably they do not trust the men to manage it properly on their own. This sequence is comically expressive of the distrust between the two sides of the family, and the final chorus of the scene makes their mutual suspicions more explicit; in asides each man expresses distrust of one of the women and each of the aunts singles out an uncle for discredit. They have each other well-weighed up, even if they are comically blind to their own faults:

'IVY:      I do not trust Charles with his confident vulgarity, acquired from worldly associates.

GERALD:   Ivy is only concerned for herself, and her credit among her shabby genteel acquaintance.

VIOLET:   Gerald is certain to make some blunder, he is useless out of the army.

CHARLES:  Violet is afraid that her status as Amy's sister will be diminished,' (I i 574-7)

Generally the two men are more benevolent than the two women. Perhaps this reflects the easier time men of their generation and rank had in the social scheme of things. Characteristically for a younger brother whose elder had inherited title and wealth, Gerald has gone into the army and absorbed the way of life of the Empire. The Monchenseys are not jockeying for prestige and they rest secure on their pedigree, perhaps complacently so. Charles talks proudly as a representative of the country gentry and claims that Amy is now one of them. Going south in winter is not Amy's style at all:

'We are country-bred people.
Amy has been too long used to our ways
Living with horses and dogs and guns
Ever to want to leave England in the winter.' (I i 23-6)

Then, unawares, he comically places himself by saying that he prefers to winter in London in the cosiness of his club, than to live up to his breeding in the wilds of Wishwood. However, while Charles hails Amy as one of his family's kind, we are to learn later from both Agatha and Amy that she is not naturally one of the Monchensey breed:

'There were many years
Before she succeeded in making terms with Wishwood'
(II ii 79-80)

'I forced myself to the purposes of Wishwood
                                             (II iii 26)

The opening dialogue of the play shows the different backgrounds of the Aunts and Uncles which fail to give them a common bond on the naturalistic level. As we shall see, it is their attempt to make conversation possible that leads them into their solecisms. We see from the dialogue the nature of the gulf between the two families that Amy had to bridge in marrying Lord Monchensey. Because Amy's experience in trying to cross the bridge was tragic, she is separated from the Uncles and Aunts, who have never really tried to do so. Hence she despises Violet and Ivy, and places no value on their advice. Agatha is her real antagonist because experience has made her a fellow sufferer.

The opening dialogue shows us the social comedy of embarrassed individuals trying to get on together in unconducive circumstances. Characteristically, after they have all embarrassed Mary with their talk of the younger generation, Violet falls to recriminations against the men:

'Really, Gerald, I must say you're very tactless,
And I think Charles might have been more considerate'.
                                             (68-9)

Despite being hurt by their conversation, it is Mary who most clearly understands how such a *faux pas* is made. In the following scene she comments to Agatha on the invidious formality of

'An official occasion of uncomfortable people
Who meet very seldom, making conversation.'
                                             (I ii 22-3)

It was because Gerald attempted to draw her into conversation, as the occasion seemed to demand, that she was hurt. He was being well-intentioned enough, but because Mary was keyed up for a personal crisis he could not have known about, she left the room – as we have seen – unable to play the social game. She was a victim of the discomfort of her elders.

The elders are also victims, as Mary's analysis of formal occasions recognises. None of them wants to be at Wishwood (I i 207-10), and reluctant guests are seldom at their best. There are the family tensions we have already discussed. Then, the Uncles and Aunts are at a further disadvantage in that for the first time since the death of Harry's wife they are to meet the widower. Because Harry is their nephew they ought to be close to him, but they know they are not. Charles confesses that he never wrote to him when his wife died and now he feels awkward about this omission (146-49). Harry, it transpires, despises his family anyway! The familiar social embarrassment of not knowing how to behave and what to say in the face of another person's bereavement is compounded by Amy's insistence that everyone should play it her way and pretend that nothing has happened. They are being put in an impossible position, one which accentuates all that is ridiculous in their characters even before Harry enters and discomforts them more. Their embarrassment is just as realistic as the deeper psychological interaction of Amy, Agatha and Mary. However, because theirs is a social uneasiness rather than a private inner agony, they can be handled in a comic mode while the others are treated with a more Ibsenesque intensity. The comedy is deliberately played off the other style to dramatic effect, and Eliot sees both the amusing side and the tragic side of such family frictions.

The dialogue of the Uncles and Aunts in the first few minutes of the play enables the audience to settle down after the heightened style of Amy's opening speech. They appear to speak about Amy as if she were not present: 'I have always told Amy she should go south in winter'. This is a device, following Agatha's sharp comment on its always being cold at Wishwood, to find a subject to talk to each other about in what would otherwise be an embarrassing void. It also distances them emotionally from Amy's presidency of the gathering. They make small talk, and in the attempt to keep up the bonhomie Charles makes his comment on Amy's being one of the Monchensey breed, which in its harmless superficiality actually misjudges her character entirely. At least it keeps the conversation going. Within a few lines they are all talking about themselves and not Amy at all. If what they reveal about themselves resembles caricature, this is consistent with the way people present themselves in situations of social embarrassment. Gerald and Violet seem to be in harmony in their criticism of the nouveau riche (40) but, as we later discover, Violet really has little regard for the Monchenseys. Charles unwittingly mocks himself, lighting a cigarette after condemning the young for losing their sense of taste and smell 'Because of their cocktails and cigarettes' (51). While the conversation continues to reveal bigoted attitudes, it is necessarily superficial, because only on the level of casual small-talk can they find any conversation at all to cover their lack of deeper intimacy. They've also felt embarrassed, doubtless, by Amy's references to death and by the tension which they do not fully understand between Agatha and Amy. Thus, although they appear to be chattering with assurance, they are superficial because they are in fact ill at ease. Yet below this social embarrassment lies a genuine bond of which they are only aware when they move from the naturalistic dialogue to speak in chorus. They share a fear of experiences which will catch them out, make them ridiculous and ill-prepared, disclose their secrets. It is in this area that the subtlety of Eliot's playing comedy against a non-comic mode can be seen.

Although they never openly discuss their discomfiture, the first choric passage (203ff) briefly unites them at a deeper level in their image of the actor's nightmare: the horror of appearing before an audience dressed in the wrong costume, lines unknown and moves unrehearsed. Their corporate panic at being found ridiculous by spectators makes the real audience's attitude to them less stereotyped. It helps us to understand their dilemma: they are people who are half-aware of their unspoken absurdity in the parts Amy has assigned to them in the social game of the reunion.

In the light of this fear of being found ridiculous by an observer, how unsettling for them must be Harry's opening lines as he moves to close the curtains:

'How can you sit in this blaze of light for all the world to
look at?
If you knew how you looked, when I saw you through the
window!

Do you like to be stared at by eyes through a window?'
(222-4)

At this moment an audience's attention is not focused directly on the Aunts and Uncles because it is Amy who replies. However, in the general uneasiness their sensitivity needs to be conveyed. Here we have a clash of different characters' conception of the truth. Objectively Harry is, as Amy points out, over-reacting: there is no need to draw the blinds in the country, besides everyone is glad to see Harry again. For Harry, however, the reality of the spirits that have been haunting him is getting stronger and stronger now that he is home. It impels him to break protocol by going to close the curtains himself rather than ring for the servants to do so (an example of Eliot's use of the social conventions of a class to economic, dramatic effect). However, none of his inner anguish can be as real to the others in the room as it is to Harry, and the Uncles and Aunts, whose chorus has just revealed their subtext to us, are bound to be wrong-footed. What they most feared has happened: they've been observed looking ridiculous. It is as if Harry has penetrated their inner anxieties.

In fact Harry has no such interest in his relatives as he is totally taken up with a paranoid horror of his own. He continues mysterious talk of eyes staring at him throughout his journey. Then, to everyone's relief, he descends to the language of conventional birthday greeting and acknowledgement of the family (241-2). Soon, enigmatic language again puts him on a separate plane, much to the confusion of everyone else: he tells them they all look 'so withered and young' (254). Then, in turn, the Uncles and Aunts attempt to rally round and do what's expected of them by Amy. Harry has touched on the subject they had tried to face earlier (187), namely it is difficult to behave as if nothing has happened. They know it has, Harry knows it has, but they come in with dutiful distractions, and perhaps gain some confidence from falling back into stereotype.

Then Amy throws the Uncles and Aunts off-balance again. Her lines produce a titter in the dress circle:

'You see your aunts and uncles are very helpful, Harry.

I have always found them forthcoming with advice
Which I have never taken.' (270-2)

However, it is important not to take Amy's words too
simply. Gerald, with his talk of riding, Charles with his
concern for the wine-cellar, Ivy with her anxiety about the
garden, and Violet with her advice for economies in the
kitchen, are all attempting to carry out the very instructions
Amy gave them: pretend nothing has happened to Harry.
They even offer advice in support of Amy's wish that Harry
should be master at Wishwood. Admittedly, Violet and Ivy
particularly adopt a kind of know-it-all tone, but they have not
deserved the ridicule that Amy pours on them for their
attempts to do as she has asked. Her comments are the more
contemptuous because spoken across the relatives to Harry,
as if inviting him to join in the joke at their expense. Their fear
of cat-calls in the gallery can only be increased. In such
circumstances, already at a disadvantage in the scene, it is
going to be all the harder for the Uncles and Aunts to make
sense of Harry. They are being made to conform to type, and
they do not like it. The choric passages show that they are
rounded people with fears wanting expression, but Amy's
control of the party prevents them ever finding their inner
voice on the naturalistic level. This is why the choric level is
dramatically essential, and in adopting it Eliot recognises the
limits of naturalistic treatment. Whether such transitions from
conversational interchanges to stylised chorus passages are
permissible within the one play is a critical issue to which I
shall return. (See chapter on The Chorus and The Furies).
    Next, Amy returns to the ground she has previously tested
twice for unsettling the relatives:

'I am an old woman.
They can give me no further advice when I'm dead.'
(275-6)

She shakes the official tone of the family dinner party by
rattling a death's head. Ivy splutters a commonplace in her
guilty embarrassment:

'Oh, dear Amy!

No one wants you to die, I'm sure!
Now that Harry's back, is the time to think of living.'
(277-9)

The initial short line implies a pause as Ivy searches for the appropriate cliché to extricate them all.

Amy is then silent for quite a while, not because reassured by Ivy, but because Harry picks up Ivy's word 'time' and proceeds to destroy the whole scene that Amy has stage-managed:

'You all of you try to talk as if nothing had happened,
And yet you are talking of nothing else.' (281-2)

He accuses them of conspiring to invent a Harry who is another person and, aware that the person he really is causes them embarrassment, he offers to leave the room. Perhaps Agatha, who has kept aloof from the whole charade, and now senses that it is not working, should move to a position on stage where Harry can engage her in a conversation that will take his inner thoughts more seriously. She reasons with him to try to help them to understand things from his point of view.

So far, Harry has spoken of his own discomfort at the way he is being treated by the family under Amy's command. At this point, however, a major development takes place which affects the way we understand the whole play. Harry now becomes judgmental about the quality of other people's lives, assuming apparently, his own extraordinary sufferings as a norm. Are we to take Harry's next lines as a statement by Eliot of Harry's superior spiritual struggles, and condone his placing of lesser mortals on a much lower rung of the ladder? Or is Harry being a prig, as Eliot later came to feel?

'But how can I explain, how can I explain to *you*?
You will understand less after I have explained it.
All that I could hope to make you understand
Is only events: not what has happened.
And people to whom nothing has ever happened
Cannot understand the unimportance of events.'
(290-6)

The problem is that, taken in themselves, these lines are quite profound. For Harry, events are external: they do not make contact with the inner person affecting the way that person exists from then on. In Harry's experience, the event of his wife's death after his unhappy marriage has affected him so deeply that it ceases to be an event: it has become an ineradicable part of his present life. It manifests itself as a sense of guilt and of being pursued by spirits of vengeance. However, in context, this profound assertion has an offensive edge. It judges the Uncles and Aunts to be people whom life has passed by only as a series of events; they are people unaltered by happenings.

Rightly, the relatives protest. Gerald splutters about 'tight corners' and 'nasty messes' (296-9), but in so doing comically confirms Harry's assessment of their lives. The clichés to which Gerald resorts in citing his days as a junior officer suggest failure on his part to contact the experience itself. However a speech of Charles a few minutes later warns us to be on our guard against taking their stereotyped expression at face value. It is Charles's reactions which highlight the nature of the conflict between Harry and the older generation. He too may sound a bit hollow in his man-of-the-world response that nothing can shock him (300-1). He may even appear caricatured in his response to Harry's feelings of guilt when the latter reveals, to the shock of the company, that he pushed his wife overboard:

> 'You mustn't indulge such dangerous fancies.
> It's only doing harm to your mother and yourself.
> Of course we know what really happened, we read it in
> the papers –
> No need to revert to it. Remember, my boy,
> I understand, your life together made it seem more
> horrible.
> There's a lot in my own past that presses on my chest
> When I wake, as I do now, early before morning.
> I understand these feelings better than you know –
> But *you* have no reason to reproach yourself.
> Your conscience can be clear.' (349-58)

This speech warrants considerable attention, for it highlights the polarity between Harry and Charles, not only in the kind of experience they have had but also in ways of handling experience. It is, in part, a generation gap. Charles is of that breed that does not discuss the personal side of life; in contrast, Harry feels impelled to expose the sordid images of which he feels his soul is constituted. The older generation, as we have seen, often suffered in silence: Amy bore her broken marriage in terrible isolation – it embittered her but it was not the kind of thing to be talked about. The whole atmosphere of the scene of the family reunion assumes that certain things are not talked about, such as Harry's wife's death. Charles is therefore making a generous gesture to Harry in admitting that he too has sorrows that press upon his chest. Being unused to personal revelations, Charles does not get the tone right, but it is more than the patronising concession which Harry takes it to be. Harry has accused the Uncles and Aunts of not knowing the 'unspoken voice of sorrow in the ancient bedroom at three o'clock in the morning' (308-9), but Charles risks admitting, in his own prosaic style, that he does wake early before morning, and feels regret and sorrow. He also ventures to offer an understanding comment on the intensity of Harry's feeling: he hints that the unhappiness of Harry's marriage made his wife's death all the more horrid. Charles is breaking Amy's taboo on this subject, and in so doing is momentarily allowed to breathe as a more rounded and compassionate human being. Finally he attempts to reassure Harry that objectively, at least, he has no cause to reproach himself. Later, when Harry has left the room, Charles hints at further unspoken depths to his life, but he maintains his guard against any personal indulgence which could be inappropriate to the conventions of his generation and his class:

'I might have done the same thing once, myself.
Nobody knows what he's likely to do
Until there's somebody he wants to get rid of'.
(431-33)

Charles's way of dealing with the unnamed personal crisis is very different from that which Harry is eventually to find through Agatha. Charles's approach is practical, and he tends to be prescriptive whereas Agatha leads Harry to self-discovery. Charles does not want Harry to become self-indulgent: it upsets mother, and 'dangerous fancies' may unbalance Harry's hold on reality. He tries reassurance in the belief that because Harry has been isolated the notion that he killed his wife has grown in his mind (402-7). Now that Harry is home, he can talk it out and reach a more rational view of the whole affair. Thus Charles offers what from his own experiences of life is a genuine interpretation of Harry's crisis and how it may be dealt with. Charles is not made ridiculous by his perspective: rather Harry, especially in his reaction to Charles, is felt by the audience to be all the more highly-strung, peculiar and convinced of being special.

What Harry responds to is not the genuine feeling in Charles's speech, but the surface level which has elements of the stock caricature which Harry despises. He misses the attempt Charles makes to loosen a lifetime's habit of silent suffering in order to help him, but catches instead the patronising tone in which Charles unfortunately expresses himself in what is, to him, an unfamiliar area of discourse. ('Remember, my boy, I understand . . .') Harry is suspicious of two things: the tone of paternal authority suggesting moral disapproval ('You mustn't indulge such dangerous fancies') and Charles's hiding behind 'events' as reported in the newspapers rather than looking for their significance. In his present mood Harry is unable to detect that, behind the crass expression, Charles is trying to relate to him sympathetically. It is a problem of communication. Harry is self-consciously trying to find words to put his experience to the family, but he is awkward and fears he will not be understood anyway:

> 'I am not speaking
> Of my own experience, but trying to give you
> Comparisons in a more familiar medium' (309-11)

he says from the pedestal of his uniqueness, to excuse his images of the 'noxious smell untraceable in the drains'. Whereas Harry speaks through images of crowded deserts, meaningless circular movement, of penetrating stains and cancer and of ghosts, Charles's language is prosaic and unspecial. Harry cannot pause to consider that Charles in his own way is also having an intolerable wrestle with words and meanings. Hampered by the conventions of his breeding, Charles's attempt to reach Harry is couched in the wrong words and sounds merely patronising and naive. Harry is ruthless:

'I knew how you would take it.
First of all you isolate the single event
As something so dreadful that it couldn't have
                                        happened,
Because you could not bear it. So you must believe
That I suffer from delusions.' (360-4)

This is not fair to the spirit of Charles's line 'your life together made it seem more horrible' (353). Just as Mary is later rebuffed by Harry for daring to suggest that she understands something of Harry's suffering, so here Charles is not credited with the ability to 'understand these things better' than Harry knows.

Eliot's skill in dramatising the Uncles and Aunts is that he allows us to see the absurdity of characters who restrict their range of emotion and expression by narrowing their lives to conventional patterns. However, he also makes the Uncles and Aunts capable of feelings which are the more poignant because they too are struggling with an experience that threatens their grip on reality, and in which we know they are being manipulated by Amy. In Charles's speech we see the boldest attempt on the naturalistic level to open up for Harry. For the others as well as for Charles, their corporate speech as chorus is the only form of deeper expression available to them, and this aspect of the play we have yet to tackle. On the comic level, the function of the Uncles and Aunts, who are battered by Amy and Harry in the process, is to throw Harry's behaviour into more objective relief. We laugh with them as they desperately try to make sense of Harry's behaviour in terms familiar to them, even if in so doing they restrict his experience. Gerald's 'God preserve us! I never thought it would be as bad as this!' (393-4) gives us a chance for welcome laughter after the highly-strung speeches of Harry. But we also know that Amy is capitalising on any laughter the Uncles and Aunts attract. Thus we are drawn towards them with some affection whereby we feel, more sharply than we otherwise might, the sting of Harry's judgment of them.

# 5

## Harry and Agatha

In discussing the Uncles and Aunts I have attempted to show that they are not to be mocked into insignificance as fools: they have a dramatic function, highlighting the hypersensitivity of Harry, and an important role in establishing the tensions within the family which Harry is intended to reunite. It is now time to see how Eliot balances against them the logic of Harry's inner truth. We have seen his behaviour in a critical light so far. An analysis of why he behaves as he does will not condone him, but will again reveal a human character established in dramatic confrontation with the other characters.

Harry's touchiness with the family appears, as we have seen, to be an arrogant assurance of his uniqueness: 'I tell you, life would be unendurable if you were wide awake' (I i 304-5). Harry responds more calmly to Agatha's attempts to illuminate his confusions, but even here he criticises the Uncles and Aunts:

> 'I think I see what you mean,
> Dimly – as you once explained the sobbing in the
>                                                 chimney
> The evil in the dark closet, which they said was not
>                                                 there,
> Which they explained away, but you explained them
> Or at least, made me cease to be afraid of them.'
>                                             (I i 388-92)

Even before his unhappy marriage, Harry had felt alienated from his relatives. The sensitive child afraid of the dark had not been taken seriously by the adults; their rationalisations failed to acknowledge that his fear was genuine. In conversation with Mary we learn that the family again failed to understand a child's imagination when they put a summer house in place of the wilderness (I ii 150ff). Thus Harry's experience of relatives is that they have never responded to him. Now, on return to Wishwood, haunted by the ghosts of a broken marriage and a guilty conscience so deep that it is almost cancerous, he anticipates their incomprehension. Almost as a defensive gesture he attacks his relatives for insensitivity before he even gives them a chance to understand.

As a boy Harry has already been wounded by the formality of his family. Indeed his marriage was an act of rebellion against his cold upbringing. The fact that he is now returning home after the failure of that marriage seems to vindicate the family traditions against his act of individuality. This makes him hypersensitive at his return. It is vital that the Uncles and Aunts are present so that the pain of returning to such a family of official relationships can be the more vividly dramatised. However, while Harry's embarrassment has inner logic to it, we have also seen enacted the logic of the relatives' embarrassment. Thus the encounter between them is not simply that of the spiritual superman exposing the inferiority of those lower down the hierarchy. It is a confrontation of people within a family seeing from the perspective of their personal experiences, which are of such different kinds that no easy understanding is going to be possible.

Furthermore, it is the dramatic logic of the play – not a spiritual theory – that demands that, of the relatives, only Agatha can minister to Harry. This is not because the other Uncles and Aunts are obtuse, but because Agatha has herself contributed to the unhappiness and bitterness which rests like a curse on the family. Just as her experience makes her the real antagonist to Amy, so it makes her the only one who can reveal the truth Harry needs to know about his father. Nor is she just an informer: Part II, scene ii must, as we have said earlier, be Agatha's confession and unburdening as well as Harry's enlightenment. She is not some sibylline guide divinely appointed by Eliot to explain hidden mysteries; she is for the first time breaking her own chosen silence of years. Thus her ministrations are essentially different from those of Charles. It is not that Charles's attempts to reassure Harry are inadequate in themselves. It is that Charles's private life, to which he alludes, in no way impinges on Harry's, and therefore, Charles's advice is inadequate. Because Agatha's private life is inextricably linked with Harry's she must be the one to unlock the door to his future.

Agatha's duologue with Harry in Part II would get nowhere if she had not already won his confidence in Part I. When in Part II she says, 'You may be afraid that I would not understand you' (ii 15), she is gently alluding to Harry's anguish immediately on his return to Wishwood. In Part I Agatha had been able to persuade Harry to relax and attempt to explain how he felt:

> 'Nevertheless, Harry, best tell us as you can:
> Talk in your own language, without stopping to
> debate
> Whether it may be too far beyond our understanding.'
> (I i 317-19)

Her tone was reassuring. Her point was that he had to hammer it out – whether or not people understood him was of only secondary importance. Thus Harry began to trust Agatha because she recognised the authenticity of his experience. She had also acted as a corrective to his arrogant expression of his sense of uniqueness. She referred there to his language; indeed, reassured by Agatha that he would be taken seriously, his language began to alter.

It is worth pausing to look at this change in his language. There is a sense in which in Part I Harry is deliberately creating an effect with startling images; there is the rhetoric of the man who sees himself in a dramatic light (see appendix):

> 'You do not know
> The noxious smell untraceable in the drains,
> Inaccessible to the plumbers, that has its hour of the
> night; you do not know
> The unspoken voice of sorrow in the ancient bed-
> room

At three o'clock in the morning.' (I i 305-9)

There is something contrived about reference to plumbers in an otherwise heightened style. Then, Harry's comparison of himself to this old house with its noxious smells (311) is again a little too self-conscious. He is aware of the awkwardness of his diction and excuses it, again in uneasy, lumpy language:

> 'I am not speaking
> Of my own experience, but trying to give you
> Comparisons in a more familiar medium.' (I i 309-11)

'I gotta use words when I talk to you' in *Sweeny Agonistes* had a greater assurance and economy.

Later Harry says, 'I talk in general terms; Because the particular has no language' (331-2). Eliot often creates poetry that denies such an assertion: contrast the assurance behind the image in *Murder in the Cathedral*. 'The torn girl trembling by the millstream'; 'trembling' is evocatively particular, and yet the phrase is expressive of a world where girls are raped and relationships seem not to exist, the world of *The Waste Land*. Perhaps Eliot is ill-at-ease with the experience he has created for Harry; perhaps the material of the play was too personal for him to handle with the necessary poetic detachment (see Biographical Postscript). However, whether or not the difficulty here is Eliot's in giving a local habitation and a name to Harry's suffering need not trouble the actor, or us, if a valid dramatic motivation can be found within the words.

Harry's difficulty in expressing himself is consistent with the view that he is baffling to *himself*, let alone to all those on stage. This Agatha understands in I i, and she encourages him to continue in his own words. With this help his imagery has moments of clarity, and he battles through to an admission of his sense of guilt at his wife's death – albeit startlingly expressed as if he murdered her. In the speech beginning at line 320 the images can still be abstract, and various ideas crowd together to suggest the jostling of his mind in its panic. 'Partial observation of one's own automatism' (327) is still heavy-handed. More sharply focused, however, is the image of the stain:

'While the slow stain sinks deeper through the skin
Tainting the flesh and discolouring the bone –
That is what matters, but it is unspeakable,
Untranslatable:' (I i 328-31)

For a few lines Harry continues to philosophise the event:

'It was only reversing the senseless direction
For a momentary rest on the burning wheel
That cloudless night in the mid-Atlantic
When I pushed her over.' (I i 335-8)

'When I pushed her over' is chillingly sparse, standing as a half-line unleashed from the cumulative pressure of the syntax through the previous three lines. The *frisson* is felt by Violet as she completes the line: 'Pushed her?' Then, as if confession of feelings of guilt has given him respite from his anguish, Harry relaxes into a lucid description of his behaviour and how he felt on deck and in the cabin after his wife drowned (339ff). It is because of Agatha's reassurance at lines 317-9 that Harry is able to talk less awkwardly, focus some of his images more precisely, and experience a moment of relief by bringing into the open his notion that he murdered his wife. Then, as we saw, Harry is thrown into turmoil again by Charles's rationale about not indulging dangerous fancies. Harry pounces on the relatives once more for their incomprehension:

'It is not my conscience,
Not my mind, that is diseased, but the world I have to live
in.' (I i 364-5)

Because at one point in their progress the women of Canterbury say that the world is utterly foul, and because Celia in *The Cocktail Party* comes to see the whole world as sinful, readers may take Harry's words here as Eliot's valuation. However, the context again shows a man being self-consciously dramatic, aware of his uniqueness, muddled by it, rejecting as useless the confused attempts of his Uncles and Aunts to help. It is again Agatha who places Harry's behaviour gently. She admits that she does not yet understand all Harry is trying to say, but also that Harry himself does not fully understand:

> 'I am also convinced
> That you only hold a fragment of the explanation.
> It is only because of what you do not understand
> That you feel the need to declare what you do.
> There is more to understand: hold fast to that
> As the way to freedom.' (I i 383-8)

It is from this point that Agatha takes up in Part II, scene ii. Harry opens by indulging in rather bitter humour at the expense of his conventional family. Arthur's accident is a 'mild' surprise that the family can cope with. He implies that his own experience is in contrast a major shock that they cannot accept. Agatha allows Harry to rail against the dulness of Wishwood and his impatience with the family. Her reply makes it clear that Eliot is not speaking through Harry to put down lesser mortals: she ignores the surface meaning of Harry's words and tries to get at the deeper discontent that she feels he is covering over in his brash and jaded talk. In eliciting from Harry what is in his mind (II ii 12-17), Agatha also hints that Harry may be afraid of being understood. She urges him not to try to explain himself so much as express himself. She implies that some of his eccentric language in Part I may have been to protect himself lest he became vulnerable through being understood. Such is the trust Agatha has managed to build up in him in Part I that he immediately responds to her now, turning away from his grouse against his relatives. Thus within the time-scale of the play she has successfully renewed his childhood trust in her ability to make him less afraid. He speaks now of being pursued by phantoms; he is anxious about what their presence means. He describes the loneliness he felt almost as soon as he married:

> 'I felt, at first, that sense of separation,
> Of isolation unredeemable, irrevocable –' (20-1)

These words are a clue to Agatha as to how to proceed: soon she is to tell Harry that his mother also felt that sense of irrevocable solitude in an unhappy marriage. Like his parents he has experienced no ecstasy and he has already begun to grasp from Dr Warburton (II i) that his parents were not happy. Harry now describes the curious sense of detachment he felt once his wife had died and he experienced himself as a murderer. The spirits which have haunted him seem to want vengeance, and they prevent him from settling down at Wishwood to forget the past trauma. He wants to know what the spirits are demanding of him. Because he feels so out of place among his family back at Wishwood he has become aware that he never was happy at home. He begins to sense that childhood unhappiness – long before his marriage – provides some deeper cause for his present misery. It is logical that this train of thought might lead him to want to know more about his father. Harry has already learnt a little from Warburton, and by the doctor's white lies (II i 74) he has deduced that Agatha knows more than has so far been revealed.

Harry's introduction of his father into the conversation is, however, rather abrupt: 'And now I want you to tell me about my father' (II ii 45). Even if Agatha had known she would eventually have to speak about her relations with Lord Monchensey, the moment when it comes may be unexpected. The actress can make effective use of the abruptness of Harry's question by having a moment to register facially the 'deeper organisation' which the question disturbs. 'What do you want to know about your father?' (46) gives her time to adjust before admitting that Harry's question can only be answered by revealing all that she has concealed behind the facade that other people – Mary for instance – found so forbidding:

'I had to fight for many years to win my disposses-
sion,
And many years to keep it. What people know me as,
The efficient principal of a women's college –
That is the surface. There is a deeper
Organisation, which your question disturbs.' (52-6)

As we begin to see the deeper Agatha we may be put off by her rather academic language: 'dispossession', 'deeper organisation', 'question disturbs'. The phrases are not particularly warm or human. However, the actress may cope with them by seeing them as a donnish garb to protect her inner self at this early stage in her revelations. She has to warm up to this major moment in her life – confessing and unburdening to Harry. The sense of taking a deep breath before the plunge may be found in the rhythm of the lines where Agatha, unusually for her, breaks the sentence in mid-line. This is most striking in:

'I will try to tell you. I hope I have the strength,' (59)

Here the two short sentences contrast her usual more self-assured, oracular style, where phrases and syntax are held in balance from one line to the next. There is a new humility in Agatha's simple broken line, and the significance of it is not lost on Harry: not for the last time in this scene he comes to see people in a new light. He had had a somewhat idealised notion of Agatha, relying on her almost as the divine saviour:

'I have thought of you as the completely strong,
The liberated from the human wheel.
So I looked to you for strength. Now I think it is
A common pursuit of liberation.' (60-3)

He is able to do here what he failed to do in response to Charles's overtures, and Mary's – to respond to the significance of what the other person is saying. He realises the importance to Agatha of what she is about to embark on. He links the liberation he is looking for with a new-found freedom for Agatha as well. Explicitly this is a scene of personal progress for Agatha as well as Harry. She is taken from her sibylline pedestal where Harry – and some critics – have placed her, as if 'liberated from the human wheel'.

In thus responding sympathetically to Agatha, Harry encourages her to go on, and her language relaxes as she gives a general background to Lord Monchensey as the country squire: beneath a considerable strength to fulfil his social role well, lay a shy, lonely man who allowed himself to be dominated by Harry's mother. Harry's response, 'There was no ecstasy' (72), is the first sign of his being able to understand his parents' unhappiness from his own experience of 'isolation unredeemable' in the first months of his own marriage.

There is then an awkwardness in the dialogue and style:

HARRY:                                          There was no ecstasy.
                Tell me now, who were my parents?
AGATHA:    Your father and your mother.
HARRY:                                          You tell me nothing.
AGATHA:    The dead man whom you have assumed to be
                                                your father.
                And my sister whom you acknowledge as your
                                                mother:
                There is no mystery here.' (72-7)

Agatha reverts to her more distant style with 'assumed to be your father', balancing 'acknowledge as your mother' and highlighting the unexpected words 'assumed' and 'acknowledge'. The emotional development of this scene requires us to take account of this strangely uncolloquial moment. Harry's realisation that there was no ecstasy in his parents' marriage seems to lead him to assume that he cannot therefore be their child, just as his own unecstatic marriage was childless. Perhaps, to him, this accounts for his feeling so different from the rest of the family: Arthur and John are, perhaps, typically uninspiring offspring of an unecstatic marriage. He senses some mystery about his birth which may be accounted for by being illegitimate. Harry finds Agatha's response evasive: 'Your father and your mother'; she has not said who in fact his father and mother were. It is at this point that Agatha's clarification takes on the more formal vocabulary and phrasing that we associate with her protective clothing as the principal of the women's college. Why should she revert to this at this moment? The actress may find the answer in the following speeches, when Agatha begins her account of falling in love with Lord Monchensey, and of protecting Harry's life by preventing Lord Monchensey from murdering the pregnant Amy. Agatha, we discover, feels herself to be Harry's mother, passionately and physically:

'If that had happened, I knew I should have carried
Death in life, death through lifetime, death in my womb.'
                                                    (115-6)

Agatha thus hardens her tone in describing who Harry's
parents were because, beneath the literal, biological truth lies
the deepest of her secrets: her womanhood had been stirred to
sexual and motherly urges which she subsequently suppressed beneath her efficient principalship. The language marks
her tension between wanting and needing to reveal the truth
to Harry and the step it involves in throwing off her protective
academic robes. She opens the way forward in her half-line,
'There is no mystery here'; this allows Harry to pursue where
– if not in the actual facts of his parentage – the mystery does
lie.

It is at this point that, for Harry's benefit, Agatha reveals
that she understands Amy's loneliness and lack of sympathy
with Wishwood. Thus she accounts for her own presence at
the house as a companion to Amy during the ill-fated
summer. She prepares for her revelation of her affair with
Lord Monchensey in her description of the summer and the
contrast with the normal coldness of Wishwood:

                                              'I remember
        A summer day of unusual heat
        For this cold country.' (89-91)

It is appropriate that Agatha never states explicitly what
happened between her and Lord Monchensey, but continues
to allude to the passion in terms of the season and climate.
The thing itself is too precious to her, and too deeply
wounding to be touched on explicitly:

        'There are hours when there seems to be no past or
                                                        future,
        Only a present moment of pointed light
        When you want to burn. When you stretch out your
                                                          hand
        To the flames.' (92-5)

The image of the hot summer blends into the heat of

passion. The language which allusively describes her affair contains also her knowledge of the ultimately destructive nature of such fire. This symbolic intensity of language can be set against Amy's reference to the affair, inviting Agatha back afterwards so that there might be 'no ugly rumours' (II iii 28); Agatha remains true to the precious quality of her destructive passion, whereas from Amy's point of view it was a sordid love affair. The poetic language Agatha uses in describing it to Harry delicately preserves the relationship between herself and Lord Monchensey, where any more direct details would debase her memory of the experience.

She continues her speech with a description of her later life of penance leading, she hopes, to another kind of fulfilment:

> 'They only come once,
> Thank God, that kind. Perhaps there is another kind,
> I believe, across a whole Thibet of broken stones
> That lie, fang up, a lifetime's march. I have believed this.
> (96-9)

The draft concluded this speech with 'I hope there is', which indicates a personal urgency to her idea that her life of self-imposed abstinence in the women's college would be penance enough to allow her later to experience another kind of ecstasy. However, her reference to God and the change of 'hope' to 'believe' brings in religious overtones that become increasingly present in the play. For Agatha the passion was illicit but valued, destructive but ecstatic – an intensity experienced but to be expiated.

Agatha continues the images of the seasons to show how she came down to earth. Autumn ended her ecstasy – too soon, because of the need to face its implications; too late because the illicit passion had happened (100ff). Wind and rain symbolise the return to Wishwood reality, yet Lord Monchensey continues to act out the dream, moving towards melodramatic plots to kill his wife. Agatha relieves the tension for herself and the audience by giving a slightly comic view of Lord Monchensey once her ecstasy was passed: 'What simple plots! He was not suited to the role of murderer' (103-4); 'a dozen foolish ways, each one abandoned, For something more ingenious'; 'He would have bungled it'(110).

The comic detachment here serves two purposes. It prepares the way for the transfer of Agatha's intensity from the summer of unusual heat to her maternal instinct for Harry. It also diverts criticism from Lord Monchensey for becoming an unbelievable melodramatic villain. He is deliberately made improbable as a murderer so that Agatha can focus on the implications rather then the reality of murder. The thought that Harry might not have been born if this fantastic murder had taken place reveals the deepest layer of Agatha's tragedy and, in her own terms, her guilt; we are being prepared for Agatha's assertion that this is no story of crime and punishment but of sin and expiation (130).

We have already seen how her speech identifying Harry in such physical terms with the life of her own womb is a poignant indication of Agatha's frustrated womanhood and sexuality (see chapter *Amy and Agatha*). Her love for Lord Monchensey, which might have borne a child, is contrasted with the bitterness of the relationship between Lord Monchensey and Amy which actually produced the child. But Agatha is not playing for sympathy: she allows herself at this crisis of confession to speak in a violently possessive way about the child she knows objectively to be none of hers: 'Something that should have been *mine* . . .' (112), 'I wanted you' (114), 'in any case I should have no other child' (118).

It may seem curious that Harry immediately accepts Agatha as a mother: 'And have me' (119); 'Everything is true in a different sense' (120). Harry's willingness to respond in fulfilment of Agatha's deepest wishes is comprehensible. She has been like a mother to him, neutralising the horrors of night-time in the nursery. She has also acknowledged the authenticity of his later experiences. Now, as he learns of the unhappy marriage into which he was born, he learns also that the father, whom he never knew, was loved, and that he himself was loved for the sake of that father – it was Agatha who provided that love. Harry feels little affection towards his real mother, and has received little from her.

He expresses the falseness of his life with relatives at Wishwood in terms of a dream:

'Perhaps my life has only been a dream
Dreamt through me by the minds of others.' (126-27)

While it is easy to see these lines as an indictment of his
mother for trying to make him live out her wishes at
Wishwood, they must also accuse Agatha, for she too has been
nurturing a dream through Harry – her dream of mother-
hood. As we have seen, this wrestling over Harry is at the root
of the renewed hostility between the two sisters. Agatha's
liability is also vital if the language of sin and expiation in her
speech is to be properly understood. Agatha acknowledges
guilt in her words: 'What we have written . . .' (129); the
passion and suffering of herself, Lord Monchensey and Amy
have led to the two women living out their dreams through the
child, denying him personal freedom. The pattern for the rest
of the scene is that, by coming to see how these dominant
women have been trying to live through him, Harry can
detach himself from them and the inhibitions they have
imposed on him.

Similarly for Agatha, opening her soul to Harry in this way
frees her from the burden of her silent penance. Thus, in the
immediate dramatic context, her language of sin and
expiation has a personal urgency:

'It is possible that you have not known what sin
You shall expiate, or whose, or why. It is certain
That the knowledge of it must precede the expiation.
It is possible that sin may strain and struggle
In its dark instinctive birth, to come to consciousness
And so find expurgation. It is possible
You are the consciousness of your unhappy family,
Its bird sent flying through the purgatorial flame.
Indeed it is possible. You may learn hereafter,
Moving alone through flames of ice, chosen
To resolve the enchantment under which we suffer.'
(131-41)

Harry himself never takes up these particular images of
religion, and it is important at this stage to see this speech as
an expression of Agatha's understanding of sin and expiation.
She is not the mouthpiece for Eliot: the dramatic context, the

penitential life Agatha has lived and the effect austerity has
had on her personal warmth, make her words a compelling
*credo* for this particular woman.

She takes comfort from the religious idea that sin may not
be confined in one person, or one act, but have communal
life.[1] Thus it is possible for one member of that community to
be the scapegoat, the one who bears the sins of the family on
his shoulders – the lightning conductor to direct the
destructive powers to earth and neutralise them. This is a
pattern already familiar in Eliot's writing in *Murder in the
Cathedral*. The images of purgatory, here, ally Agatha's
religion to Catholic Christianity, and her confidence that
knowledge of the sin must precede expiation places her view
within the doctrine that the scapegoat must be a willing
sacrifice, knowing what he is taking on.

Agatha expresses her religious perspective in terms of
possibility, not of certainty: the phrase 'it is possible' recurs
through the speech. She is suggesting to Harry that he may
take up willingly the burden of the family's guilt, but behind
the repetitions is the urgency of personal hope: her own sense
of relief from guilt depends upon whether Harry will take on
himself this saintly responsibility. This is her concept of truth;
whether Harry is to see his destiny in quite these terms we
shall consider later, but for Agatha it is an act of religious faith.
Her revelation of Harry's past, therefore, has been a huge
risk.

Agatha is exhausted by the scene, and her language is quite
different from the oracular style she adopted earlier in the
play. There is a humility as she describes her feelings. She is
tired for two reasons. In the first place, because of the nature
of her faith, she knows that an effort is needed on her part to
create a new life for herself. It is with some tragic insight that
she now views the life she has led as one of spiritual
poverty:

> 'It is as if
> I had been living all these years upon my capital,
> Instead of earning my spiritual income daily:
> And I am old, to start again to make my living.'
> (152-5)

A second reason for her tiredness is that she has already begun the action necessary to renew herself spiritually. She has confessed her deepest secret. She has, within her concept of faith, revealed the sin not only of herself but of the unloving family into which Harry was born. It would be reasonable for the actress to assume a weariness from the release of the tension of bearing that burden in silence and alone for so many years. Agatha is now 'a little frightened' (160), presumably not knowing how she'll cope in her new spiritual circumstances, but also because she does not yet know how Harry will react to the full implications of her faith.

There is, however, one thing that might disturb us about her faith: does it smack of passing the buck? It is hardly Harry's fault that the adults have tried to live their dreams through him, yet he is being asked to bear all the burdens to help ease the conscience of those who have wronged him. We may feel that Agatha is lucky to get away with this, for in a new sense she is still living through Harry.

It is now that Harry's reaction becomes important. The salvation that Agatha hopes for through Harry's taking up the family burden is also, it seems, a salvation for Harry himself; it meets his own experience and makes sense of the ghosts that have been pursuing him. Gradually Agatha's revelations about his past, which have personal depth for her, also remove clouds from Harry's own bewilderment and give a fuller perspective on his feelings of guilt arising from his own loveless marriage. As we have seen, Agatha's language of sin and expiation follows upon Harry's acceptance of her motherly feelings towards him. In other words, she only takes the great risk of asking Harry to take on the family responsibility after she has been reassured of Harry's instinctive response to her deepest feelings. Agatha's revelations of her part in his past have brought him, at last, to countenance the idea that he only dreamt he pushed his wife overboard. Thus his own guilt becomes eased. His response to her suggestion that he may become the family's bird sent flying through the purgatorial flame is to feel uplifted and happy:

'It is as if happiness
Did not consist in getting what one wanted

Or in getting rid of what can't be got rid of
But in a different vision.' (145-48)

For the first time in the play Harry's speech really relaxes;
the rhythm becomes conversational, the language colloquial.
What is not yet clear is whether Harry's lightness of heart
comes from finding liberation through Agatha's religious
view, or whether his different vision comes from the
revelation that his inhibiting family is not what he had taken it
to be. The emphasis of his next major speech (163ff) suggests
that it is seeing his family as human beings for the first time
that is uppermost in his mind. He does not take up the
religious language, but responds to Agatha on a human
level:

'You frightened! I can hardly imagine it!' (161)

Harry again sees Agatha anew, no longer the 'completely
strong', the 'liberated from the human wheel'. Agatha's
revelations show her to have been spun vigorously on the
human wheel, and bound to it in her subsequent life. Harry
only now begins to have some understanding of Agatha and
the whole family. He uses imagery of theatre and acting to
convey how he saw the family's formality. For the first time, he
sees as flawed the family that so terrified him by its
obligations:

'But it is very odd:
When other people seemed so strong, their apparent
                                                  strength
Stifled my decision.' (171-3)

Primarily, as his next lines are to show, Harry is thinking of
his mother's dominant will. However, his earlier reference to
Agatha as 'the completely strong' suggests that she too has had
a part in stifling him, and that her confession also releases him
from subservience to her strength of will.
The next two and a half lines, when Harry focuses on his
mother, are at the heart of the play from his point of view:

'Now I see

I might even have become fonder of my mother –
More compassionate at least – by understanding.'
(173-5)

The layers here need unskinning. First, there is regret that it was not possible for him to have known earlier all he now knows – 'I wish I had known – but that was impossible' (162). He therefore regrets the way he has treated his mother. The words 'fonder' and 'compassionate' place his comment in contrast to that lack of family affection which he has felt. He now sees that the 'formal obligation' which had replaced 'family affection' at Wishwood was to cover up the wounded feelings that Amy was unable to face.

The audience responds warmly to Harry here, perhaps for the first time. As he is now able to cast off his self-centredness he begins to tune into the complexity of other characters' lives. Since Eliot's dramatisation of the frictions of the family reunion has gradually revealed to us depths in each character, we are relieved that Harry is coming to a more generous, rounded perception of his mother, at least. Harry feels that, if he had understood that Amy was miserable and that her own need for consolation compelled her to force on him the role of future master of Wishwood, he could have coped better. He could have loved her rather than turned against her. Understanding would have given him the safety of a kind of detachment whereby his emotions would not have been trapped beneath her dominance.

However, even at this moment of relief comes the start of a further painful development. Harry rejects the idea that he could have been fonder, or at least more compassionate because, he feels, 'she would not like that' (176). The tragic implications of this line are hardly noticeable here, but the ensuing scenes with Amy might have taken a very different turn if Harry had felt able to show his mother that he understood and could have affection for her. To this we will return.

At this stage the audience is swept along by the happiness of Harry's sense of release. He develops his earlier inkling that his life has been a dream, dreamt through him by the minds of others. He has been wounded in a war of phantoms – the damage was done by the adoption of formal roles, not so much by the human beings playing them. His new knowledge of the family makes his previous understanding of them unreal; his image of shadows and phantoms here prepares for a shift in emphasis to the spirits that have been haunting him since his wife's drowning. There follows another line of great significance:

> 'The things I thought were real are shadows, and the
> real
> Are what I thought were private shadows. O that awful
> privacy
> Of the insane mind! Now I can live in public.' (179-81).

The crucial line – also one of the most memorable for its simplicity yet richness of implication – is 'O that awful privacy of the insane mind!' This line has the power to reach from the particular of Harry's experience to the universal. It puts us in the position of those we judge as insane: they have a logic not inaccessible to themselves although it appears lunatic to observers.

This line also has the power of throwing into relief Harry's behaviour in Part I, and it makes us reassess the reactions of the Uncles and Aunts. Harry now reveals that his greatest fear had been that he was indeed mad. Everything around him in the staged scene on his return had reinforced his lack of confidence in his private world. Yet another layer of self-protection can now be seen in his earlier reactions to the Uncles and Aunts: the actor playing Harry can take this line as part of the reason for his irritation at Charles's warning, 'You mustn't indulge such dangerous fancies'. It is because this is precisely what Harry himself feared he was doing that his reaction was so sharp: 'You must believe that I suffer from delusions'. He blamed the Uncles' and Aunts' supposed narrowness, rather than acknowledge that he too feared what they fear about him. Thus Ivy also becomes less of a banal plodder in her lines:

> 'But I understand –
> I have heard of such cases before – that people in his
> condition
> Often betray the most immoderate resentment

At such a suggestion.' (ie that they should see a doctor)
              'They can be very cunning –
Their malady makes them so. They do not want to be
                                                cured
And they know what you are thinking' (I i 396-401)

Ivy's tone was defensive as she tried to cope with Harry by
pigeon-holing him as 'one of those types' she's heard of, but
the essence of what she said is correct. If Harry feared he was
insane, his need to put Charles in the wrong was activated by
the need to protect himself from facing the fear. Charles's
insight,

'I suspect it is simply that the wish to get rid of her
Makes him believe he did.' (I i 404-5)

is also later vindicated by Harry's, 'Perhaps I only dreamt I
pushed her'.

Harry has now had from Agatha the knowledge that
liberates him from his misunderstanding of his family. Apart
from its cleansing effect on Agatha herself, her exploration
has provided Harry with the evidence he has been seeking of
the origin of wretchedness behind his meagre childhood. The
search for some deeper origin than his broken marriage has
been intensified since his return to Wishwood by the pressure
of the Furies at the very place he had expected to escape them.
If Harry is not mad, these private shadows need objective
reinforcement in the play, and Agatha's explanation has
relieved Harry from madness by disclosing the origin of
wretchedness that made the Furies fiercest at home. Harry's
own experience of a loveless marriage, of guilt at his wife's
death, of fear that he might have murdered her, are now seen
by him to match the pattern of his ancestors' misery. It is
because he is able to equate his own and his parents' tragedies
that Agatha's explanations are so acceptable to him.

Eliot came to criticise the 'aria' passages in the play for not
arising out of character and situation. The duet that now
follows between Agatha and Harry can, I feel, be justified
dramatically. We have seen how in the preceding duologue
Harry needed Agatha's explanation, and how Agatha needed
to reveal the past to Harry. The progress of the two characters

is mutual and the stage they reach is one of closeness, not necessarily in rationale, but in depth of relationship in sharing secrets and fears. The duet sums up the respective hells the two characters have lived in till the moment of purgation. The images are symbolic, but they have their validity in the particular experiences that we have unfolded for us in the play. Agatha's glimpse of fulfilment in her passion for Lord Monchensey finds itself in the image of the little door into the rose garden, but the black raven blots out light and joy; her life of penance begins in images of feet scraping harshly on stone corridors. It is the image of cold, meaningless movement that balances Harry's resumption of his image of shrieking noises in his circular desert. These were their phantom selves; now they have entered a new rose garden where, through their openness to each other and through Agatha's confession of love and renunciation, they have found their true selves. The sense of communion they have in their duet is a fulfilment of a loving relationship driven underground in both their lives. It is not sexual, nor is it now particularly surrogate mother-and-son. Now that her possessive love for Harry has been confessed, it matures to that of two adults experiencing the relief of bringing their sufferings to each other in trust. After this lyrical expression of the implications of the dialogue which preceded it, when Harry experiences the Eumenides again he can now accept the Furies as external guides rather than internal phantoms of guilt.

Having examined the family dimension of Harry's new vision, we can move to the religious dimension and see how his acceptance of the phantoms as guides relates to, or is different from, Agatha's vision of Harry as the family's bird sent flying through the purgatorial flame. Previous imagery of the noxious smell in the drains is replaced by 'a communication, a scent Direct to the brain' (I ii 228-9). The Furies which he had feared were figments of his insane imagination are now manifest. Their objective presence is later confirmed by Mary, Agatha and Downing. This means that any danger there might be of Agatha using Harry for her personal view of family salvation is neutralised by Eliot: Harry has his own guides apart from her. This becomes Agatha's life-line in defending herself from Amy's charge that she has bewitched Harry.

The message of the Furies becomes clear to Harry only after Agatha has helped him to see his past in perspective and to see why a return to the life patterned for him at Wishwood would be impossible. He cannot be enmeshed in the family because this would prevent him from realising his own potential, wherever that is to be. He knows the Furies are ready to leave Wishwood (235) and he determines to follow them without delay. He feels that his own suffering has left him befouled, but he believes that following the guidance of the Furies is the only 'way out of defilement – which leads in the end to reconciliation' (279-80). While Agatha hopes that Harry may come to see himself as removing the curse from the family, Harry at this stage still sees the departure from Wishwood in terms of personal cleansing from the guilt he has felt in his own life. He does not see himself as clearly as Agatha does, as the inheritor of a family stain of lovelessness.

It is important that there should be this difference of perspective. Harry is able to tell his mother, in all honesty, that his decision to leave Wishwood is not of Agatha's making: 'My advice has come from quite a different quarter' (289). Indeed, he asserts his independence of Agatha more personally. In reply to Amy's resentment that Agatha and not she should know why he is going, Harry says:

'I do not know whether Agatha knows
Or how much she knows. Any knowledge she may
                                        have –
It was not I who told her . . .' (302-4)

The reason he feels impelled to follow his spiritual guides is that they have been the ones to drive him to find out why he cannot find sanity by remaining at Wishwood. They were the supernatural agents of the quest: Agatha provided the human explanations by showing the truth of Wishwood which had been concealed beneath the polite formalities.

Then, in a vague way, he suggests that he may go into some kind of spiritual life. He adopts the imagery of religious asceticism and mission:

'To worship in the desert, the thirst and deprivation,
A stony sanctuary and a primitive altar,

The heat of the sun and the icy vigil,
A care over the lives of humble people . . .' (331-4)

He feels elected to a special life and says he does not
understand why he was chosen for it. Thus Harry sees his
departure as a supernatural calling to a religious life: it is the
only way of life that seems to make sense of the confusion he
has experienced. It relates to Agatha's talk of sin and
expiation, in that he feels that only by denying himself the
expected and conventional fulfilments will he cleanse himself
from his feeling of guilt, and ultimately be reconciled to those
from whom he has been estranged (280). Perhaps the closest
he comes to seeing his mission in Agatha's terms, as taking on
the responsibility of exorcising the curse on the family, is
where he announces that he wants John to take over mastery
at Wishwood:

'What would destroy me will be life for John,
I am responsible for him.' (340-41).

# 6

## The Effect on Amy and Mary
## of Harry's Departure

Were Eliot to have made the Eumenides a kind of *deus ex machina* there would be cause for discomfort: a play which had explored so profoundly the subtext beneath the social act performed at Wishwood – and had used devices of great naturalistic playwrights to do so – would appear to contradict its style by putting the ultimate solution on a mystical level and leaving it at that. All that happens after Harry's 'I shall be safe with them; I am not safe here' (II ii 317-8) would, as Donoghue argues[1], be formally redundant. Apart from Amy dying there would be nothing 'essential to the dramatic pattern'. But there is much more to Harry's final scene with his mother than is included in Donoghue's conception of the play's dramatic pattern. Harry's scene with his mother, after he has accepted the supernatural call, is crucial in placing this vocation in perspective. The solution to leave does not simply over-ride all that has gone before. Harry's sense of super-natural reality is dramatised as being in conflict with the human call. Dedicating his life to the demands of spiritual beings is seen in the context of its human cost and even of its contribution to human hurt and tragedy.

On the human level, Harry's crucial scene with Agatha has shown that to reach reconciliation people must be prepared to strip away the paraphernalia of habitual behaviour, behaviour which is based on assumptions and misunderstandings about one another. On the human level, a reconciliation between Harry and his mother would entail some similarly open encounter between them. This Harry feels is impossible: 'But she would not like that' (II ii 176).

Agatha seems to have encouraged Harry's point of view by implying that he should leave without trying to reach any understanding or reconciliation with Amy; he is on a treasure hunt with a vital clue and must waste no time in leaving:

> 'Love compels cruelty
> To those who do not understand love.
> What you have wished to know, what you have
> learned
> Mean the end of a relation, make it impossible.
> You did not intend this, I did not intend it,
> No one intended it, but . . . You must go.' (II ii 266-71)

Despite our understanding of the tragedy in Agatha's life, despite the wisdom experience has taught her and which she imparts to Harry, and despite the vindication of her religious insight by the call of the Furies, we in the audience, like Amy and the Uncles and Aunts, can never feel comfortable about her. Here we are uneasy that her judgment is coloured by her own experience of Amy and the impossibility we diagnosed of Amy and Agatha being reconciled in human terms. We may wonder whether Agatha and Harry underestimate Amy's capacity for responding to an overture of affection which might lead to deeper self-discoveries in reconciliation.

Certainly the situation presented to us in the play offers Harry no context for such an overture. However, in the scene between Harry and Amy (II ii 282ff), the audience experiences a tension akin to that tension crucial to tragedy: we long for one thing, knowing that the other will happen. Harry does try to speak kindly to his mother: 'Oh, mother, This is not to do with Agatha' (287-8), and seems genuinely concerned that Amy should recognise the personal nature of his decision to leave and not attribute it in ancient enmity to Agatha. There is a gentleness also in, 'I can only speak . . . to tell you that I would have liked to explain' (298-300) and the compassionate recognition, 'It is hard for you too, mother, it is indeed harder, Not to understand', an insight which comes from his own experience of days when he misunderstood his family. We feel that Harry here is on the edge of opening up to Amy; intimacy seems almost possible. But Harry speaks all the time on the assumption that she cannot make sense of him: 'I can only speak / And you cannot hear me' (297-8).

Once again the problem is that Harry cannot find the language in which to explain. What he needs here is a short-cut for the much longer, painful experience of trying to rebuild the relationship on honest ground. He knows enough, perhaps, to try, but Amy still clings to her protective lie and does not face publicly – even with one close to her – the deep wounds she has suffered. Harry resorts to language that has currency with us because we have witnessed the logic of his commitment to a religious solution, but his imagery must remain baffling to Amy. In answer to her repeated request to know why he is going he speaks of being in flight, of being in ignorance of invisible pursuers, and then refers to his whole life as a flight and tells her that phantoms fed on him while he fled (302ff). Harry does not explain to her what the word 'phantom' has come to mean to him – how it expresses the false, formal surface life of Wishwood, the inhumane routine covering those human hurts too deep to bare openly. He does not reveal that he understands what his mother has been through; she is expected to do all the comprehending unaided. Even now, there is in Harry something of the sense of being unique. He talks to Amy next of spectres, his special guides and, rightly, Amy cannot accept such an explanation. She is not obtuse to relate his words to the literal level:

'There is no one here!
No one, but your family!' (311-12)

Harry has failed to help her see the reality that the metaphorical language has for him; she can only respond on a literal plane. Harry does not respond to her genuine failure to grasp his allusive meaning. He also fails to connect with her in his attempt to explain the difference between running away from reality and facing it (312ff). Amy still sees his decision as 'running away'.

Agatha then attempts to explain, but her voice has the bitterness which her relationship with Amy always provokes:

'In a world of fugitives

> The person taking the opposite direction
> Will appear to run away.' (319-21)

Epigrammatic, pithy but, in the dramatic context, almost calculated to antagonise. Sure enough, Amy resents the clever intrusion: 'I was speaking to Harry.' Agatha's comment is put forcefully out of court: this is a dialogue between mother and son. Harry continues by relying on his new perspective on sanity and he can see that this must seem madness to other people. But he has given Amy none of the context whereby this language of sanity and insanity makes sense. It is not surprising if she feels that there is a conspiracy between Agatha and Harry: as we have seen, although Agatha does not make Harry's decision for him, he could not have decided without her. Thus Amy has the disadvantage. Whatever attempt Harry makes to protect Agatha from Amy's wrath over his decision, the fact remains that he and his aunt share a context whereby his images make sense. Amy does not. She is right if she feels excluded.

Harry then describes where he will go in missionary images, but he himself is vague as to what the future holds. It is the decision to go that is vital for him dramatically.

Whatever Eliot may originally have thought about the rightness of Harry's response to the religious calling, his writing in this scene between Amy and Harry, with the telling intrusion of Agatha, is such that it arouses the audience's feeling of pity for Amy. Here Eliot holds the balance between the salvation of the son and the tragedy of the mother to superb effect; this prepares the way for us to criticise Harry for allowing the supernatural call to overrule his human responsibilities to those close to him.

The scene which follows this, between Agatha and Amy, achieves no reconciliation between the two women. With the news that Mary also intends to depart, Amy concludes the sequence in bitter recognition that her purposes have been destroyed: she identifies these with the house that can be left to crumble (II iii 123ff). However, the confrontation with Agatha has brought into the open the pain of the relationship between them and the origin of that pain in the unhappiness of Amy's marriage. A process of honesty has begun, even if, in this case, it is in a scene of deep bitterness. Without this scene with Agatha, it is doubtful whether Amy would have the momentary and partial insight that she expresses just before her death:

> 'At my age, I only just begin to apprehend the truth
> About things too late to mend: and that is to be old.
> Nevertheless, I am glad if I can come to know them.
> I always wanted too much for my children,
> More than life can give. And now I am punished for it.'
>
> (II iii 186-90)

Although the damage in her relationship with Agatha has been too deep to heal, it seems, from Amy's insight here, that a reconciliation with Harry might be possible. But he has gone and, as the doctor warned, a sudden shock could kill her: she dies a few moments later. There is a new and momentary humility here. Instead of self-pitying attempts to unnerve the Uncles and Aunts with her earlier talk of chilly deaths in vacant rooms, Amy here faces a tragic aspect of old age – the apprehension too late of the truth about things that cannot be mended. Her comments on what she wanted from her children are the beginnings of a realisation; her children became the agents whereby she forced herself to the needs of Wishwood after her marriage had failed to fulfil her. The explosion of the tensions between her and Agatha at the start of the scene is crucial to the dramatic pattern; the brutality of the exposure of each woman by the other has shaken to the front of Amy's consciousness the truth about her miserable marriage, which her life of formal family obligations had pushed to the back of her mind. Because Harry could not explain himself at a deep enough level, and because Amy herself could not open up to him at such a deep level until too late, she sees his departure now as a punishment to her. His departure is not accepted in a loving context, but she sees it as a kind of retribution. Thus, Amy's moment of insight becomes all the more tragic in that it does not lead to reconciliation in human terms, rather to further bitterness. The harshness returns immediately in her contempt for her brothers and sisters, the ill-used Uncles and Aunts, as she asks Gerald and Violet to take her into the other room. There she dies a few moments later, with the line echoing her earlier panic in the face of death:

> 'Agatha! Mary! come!
> The clock has stopped in the dark!' (267-8)

Amy's death, the momentary insight and the redoubled bitterness of self-reproach are a crucial balance to Harry's decision to go. We are not left with a neat religious panacea whereby the other characters are seen to be inadequate or their final scenes redundant (Donoghue). Rather, Amy's death highlights the pain of the failure of reconciliation on the human level.

The other character close to Harry, who is wounded by his departure, is Mary. She comes to accept that she must let him go. She is part of the web of Wishwood that would trap him; she too has been dreaming her life through him, but not to such sinister effect as Amy and Agatha. She ends the play with a more realistic understanding of herself, but this understanding provides no human outlet for her loving qualities which we have warmed to earlier in the play. She awakened to awareness of tragic waste:

> 'You remember what I said to you this evening?
> I knew that I was right: you made me wait for this –
> Only for this. I suppose I did not really mean it
> Then, but I mean it now. Of course it was much too late
> Then, for anything to come for me: I should have known it;
> It was all over, I believe, before it began;
> But I deceived myself. It takes so many years
> To learn that one is dead!' (114-21)

Mary looks to Agatha, as she did in I ii, for help in finding a job away from Wishwood. But her perspective now is different: while she sensed earlier that it was right for her to go, it is only now that she is really committed to the idea of leaving. Earlier, as we saw, wanting to go was a kind of evasion of meeting Harry again and rekindling knotted memories and desires. Now her experience in the course of the play has shown her that there can be no future in her relationship with

Harry and any hopes at the start of the play were a deception. She realises that her womanhood is dead and that, in fact, it died years ago.

While Mary's new awareness comes in part from having her tenderness towards Harry so cruelly rebuffed in I ii, it comes also from what Agatha now has to tell her about the kindly nature of the Furies and the supernatural design that makes Harry's departure purposeful. It is here that Eliot's dramatic footing falters; the former awareness he has dramatised compellingly but the latter relies too much on Agatha's mere moral assertion. The scene is hard to play because Eliot seems to rush the development.

Certainly the episode is much better than it was in draft form, where Eliot first gave Mary a lengthy, petulant grouse at Amy for treating her so inconsiderately, and then a cheaply sarcastic speech to Agatha, claiming Mary can follow her example by becoming a teacher and being unpleasant to women:

> 'And I've had enough of being petted, patronised and
> bullied
> By older women. Now I want my own turn.'[2]

Eliot drops that passage as inappropriate to his final, subtler characterisation of Mary. Instead Mary's preoccupation in the final version is focused where the dramatic logic requires it to be – on Harry. Her entry in II iii is occasioned by news from Denman that Harry is to leave. Mary's fear is that the Furies who so terrified Harry – with such painful consequences for herself – will now pursue him to his destruction.

We have hardly seen Mary on stage since Harry's rejection of her in Part I scene ii. Her difficulty in coping with Agatha's austerity is economically recaptured by Eliot:

> 'He is in great danger, I know that, don't ask me,
> You would not believe me, but I tell you I know.'
> (II iii 87-8)

The audience has by now adjusted to the deeper Agatha that Mary has not come to understand, and in the half-line,

'You would not believe me', Eliot effectively reminds us of
Mary's opinion of Agatha as unsympathetic. Similarly Mary
cannot know that Harry has come to accept the Furies as
guides, thus the first development in the scene is for her to be
reassured about their purpose. Where Eliot loosens his
dramatic grip is that, in explaining Harry's departure, Agatha
relies on *our* knowledge of how she has come to this
interpretation of events. Eliot lets this suffice, instead of
dramatising the process whereby Mary can also come to
acknowledge it as a meaningful interpretation. Such a
discrepancy could only work dramatically if Mary, like Amy
with Harry, never really accepts that he must go.

The energy in Mary's speech comes from her concern for
Harry. The pace is almost breathless: she cannot pause to
explain. She willingly gives up her own concerns about
whether to stay or leave Wishwood, wanting only what is best
for Harry – an indication of the self-effacing nature of her love
for him, despite his rebuff:

> 'I will stay or I will go, whichever is better;
> I do not care what happens to me,
> But Harry must not go . . .' (92-4)

The desperate personal urgency behind these words is
consistent with what we have seen of her relationship with
Harry. Her experience of the Furies makes her convinced that
Harry is safest at Wishwood, and she is in near-panic, wanting
him to be helped and protected from them at all costs.

Agatha then reinterprets the Furies to her, and Mary stops
in her tracks:

> 'Oh! . . .so . . .*you* have seen them too!' (108)

Her desperation subsides in the surprise and relief
indicated by the hesitations. However, Eliot makes this line do
too much work at a crucial moment in Mary's development. It
is all the more taxing for the actress and audience because the
line is about the Furies whose role in the play is a tricky one at
the best of times. First of all, this line is the only indication
Eliot gives us in the script that Mary has seen the Furies, thus
suggesting that her denial of their presence with Harry was to

try to comfort him. The actress will need to have conveyed this by her physical demeanour and reaction on stage at that time; only then can this line ring true. The line is also an expression of relief that she does not have to bear her experience of the Furies alone any more – Agatha has seen them too. What's more, she need not fear that Agatha would not believe her about the spirits after all. There is the beginning of a shared experience here that makes the development of an understanding between the two women possible. The trouble is that Eliot assumes too much.

Despite the weight this line has to bear, Eliot manages to keep the focus in his presentation of Mary precise. After Agatha's fifteen lines of reassurance (95-108) Mary does not move immediately from her hysterical entry to complete acceptance of Agatha's account of Harry's destiny. The main effect of the speech has been to allay her fears about the Furies, not to inform her about the finer points of Harry's new life. In Mary's state it would be implausible for her to make immediate sense of Agatha's talk of Harry being specially elected by the powers of the other world, of his being guided across the frontier by the Furies, of a distinction between people whose life exists only in this world and not in the other, of the new meaning Harry's life now gives to such words as danger and safety.

Nonetheless, it does seem part of the dramatic pattern of the play that Mary does absorb Agatha's rationale of Harry's departure. Mary is later to join with Agatha in the ritual of blowing out the candles on Amy's birthday cake. There, at the end of the play, she shares the verse form, the language and imagery used by Agatha – the image of the curse by which Agatha made explicable to herself and Harry the tragedy of their lives at Wishwood (II ii 241ff). Such images, which make sense in the light of Agatha's experience, are new to Mary, and have not been given currency in the context of Mary's growth in understanding. Certainly their final poetic rapport establishes strikingly that a bond between Mary and Agatha has been achieved by the end of the play. Such a bond is comprehensible in that both are lonely victims of frustrated human love; they want the best for Harry, and they want the tragedy of the family to receive some eventual resolution. Experience has shown them that their human endeavours are limited, and their chant together, and their movements in the ritual circle, suggest that they both put their faith in powers beyond to achieve the final resolution. The question which troubles us is whether Eliot hasn't short-circuited his dramatic method to achieve this bond. The poetic duet shows authorial intention, but the exchange between Mary and Agatha in II iii cuts short the stages by which, elsewhere, Eliot has developed his characters through the duologues we have examined.

We notice the sharpest jolt when Mary begins her speech, 'Then you will help me!' (113). Agatha has just spoken of each person having their own direction to follow. She has defined Harry's calling, but says that she and Mary may meet again:

'In our wanderings in the neutral territory
Between two worlds.' (112-3)

Mary takes this to be an offer of practical help with finding a job outside Wishwood. The jump here from Agatha's metaphysical discussion of 'here' and 'elsewhere' (95) and of wandering between 'two worlds', to Mary's far more practical concern of needing help in finding a fellowship is a hard one. For Mary 'here' and 'elsewhere' have been much more geographical than for Agatha: 'here' meant Wishwood, 'elsewhere' meant beyond the gatehouse (91). It is hard for the actress playing Mary to relate Agatha's metaphysics and her imagery of being between two worlds to Mary's everyday concerns in the dialogue.

Things are made much more complicated by a further layer in Mary's speech. The actress has too little time given her to make credible her acceptance of Agatha's explanation of Harry's departure. Implied in Mary's speech is that she accepts the validity of letting Harry go. Only because she has accepted his destiny as separate from hers can she realise that she has deceived herself in hoping for Harry. The only way she can have come to accept this separation as something positive is by endorsing Agatha's interpretation of events. We have seen how the dramatic situation meant that Mary could not reasonably have absorbed all Agatha had said. Now, however, in the space of a few lines, she accepts the moral saying-so of Agatha without having had the necessity of

Harry's departure authenticated in her own dramatic experience within the play. The weakness of Eliot's rushing things here is the more striking because he has been meticulous in the detailed exposition of developments in other relationships in the play. It leads critics towards the conclusion that Eliot sees Mary as intuitively higher up the spiritual scale than Amy, but not as advanced as Agatha: Mary has grasped the meaning without the experience to authenticate Agatha's language and interpretation, whereas Amy failed to make such an imaginative leap when Harry's language failed to connect with her experience. However, I have argued that Amy's failure is dramatically effective in showing Harry's inability to express the sympathy he feels with his mother; Amy's failure in spiritual terms at that point was matched by Harry's failure in human terms. With Mary the problem does not have such a compelling resolution. Eliot has hurried what could have been a more careful development. Mary is halfway there in that (in I ii) she has discovered that the relationship with Harry has no future; she has also seen the Furies; all she needs is time to digest credibly, within Eliot's naturalistic characterisation, the interpretation which can  make these events meaningful to her.

Again, at the start of this sequence between Mary and Agatha, Eliot has relied on poetic echo to establish the situation. Agatha defends her behaviour with Harry: 'I have only watched and waited' (II iii 82). This recalls for us the advice that Mary found so infuriating in I ii. It is designed to highlight the change that is about to come in Mary's perception, finding that Agatha's advice was right after all: 'You made me wait for this – Only for this' (115-6). Similarly her half-line – 'Then you *will* help me!' (113) balances her earlier disappointment, 'So you will not help me!' (I ii 83). However the poetic nuance of 'I have only watched and waited' actually falsifies the dramatic truth, for Agatha does much more: she has spoken, confessed and revealed her own urgent need for salvation. Is Agatha suddenly untrue to herself, and Eliot untrue to his characterisation of her?

We come up against a fundamental problem in the presentation of Agatha. She is a woman of considerable wisdom with a capacity for understanding something of religious mysteries. It is she, as here with Mary, who does most of the interpreting of events within the supernatural design. It is not surprising that critics see her as a quasi-priestess. She may very easily be taken as the mouthpiece for Eliot were it not that the play, which sustains her life as a character, does not create her so unambiguously. Agatha is a sinner desperate for forgiveness. She places her faith in a religious outcome whereby Harry wins salvation for her and the family. We have seen how earlier, to cope with her sin, she had elected to live in a manner which cut out close personal relationship. Eliot has dramatised a tragic woman. The problem arises because Agatha's interpretation of the spiritual significance of events is founded in a morally ambiguous position as a human being. Her view of religion is coloured by her personal need to cut herself off from human relationships and by a scepticism about the effectiveness of human endeavours. She therefore discourages Harry from prolonging his relationships at Wishwood; the tragic reper-cussions of this advice we have just discussed in the case of Amy. We can admit that the Furies give Harry's calling necessary objectivity beyond Agatha's interpretation, but we only have Agatha's word that following the Furies requires such urgent severing of the human ties. Harry must follow the bright angels, but must this entail insensitivity – even cruelty – to the human beings closest to him? Agatha puts us on edge because she certainly does not discourage this insensitivity, and may even be felt to contribute to it. We wonder now how comfortable Mary will be with Agatha as her helper. In Agatha, Eliot has dramatised a tragic but not particularly nice person and we may remain sceptical about whether her influence is wholly altruistic. The play does not suffer because of this doubt. Rather it becomes a much more realistic exploration of the human tensions involved in seeking out, explaining or coming to terms with a religious calling. It is the dramatisation of these tensions which, I am arguing, makes the play powerful and moving.

There remains for the actress the problem of how to interpret the part in her scene with Mary in such a way that her ambiguity can be conveyed to the audience. She needs to explore the subtext which provides the motivation to make this scene consistent with the character she has played till now.

Mary has just come on stage in the middle of the row between Amy and Agatha. Amy tries to continue the row in the presence of this new audience, and accuses Agatha of being unscrupulous and of casting spells on Lord Monchensey and Harry. Agatha is under pressure in the presence of her former student, whom she may not want to embarrass with the sisters' conflict and before whom she stands to lose her dignity. Agatha withdraws from her exposed passions and adopts her defensive, sibylline tones again:

'I have only watched and waited. In this world
It is inexplicable, the resolution is in another.' (82-3)

'I have only watched and waited' gives Agatha the authority of an observer of the events which the Furies have brought about. The words deliberately omit the personal investment that Agatha has in Harry's decision. There is no reason, after all, why, just because she has revealed so much to Harry in a scene of special intimacy, she should wear her heart upon her sleeve on all occasions. Agatha reverts to the formality of the college principal.

Having introduced the notion of two worlds, Agatha further exonerates herself from Amy's accusations by saying that she would never tempt a person across the frontier into that other world if he was destined merely to live in this world. Harry was led across the frontier by the Furies, and she says that her interpretation is based on what she has herself learned from seeing the Furies. Her speech implies that there are those who are elected and those who are not, and it seems to express the dualism in Eliot that critics have found distasteful. But her speech must be placed by what we know she has omitted, the fact that Harry's taking on the call of the Furies had a personal urgency for her. The dramatic situation makes her assume a greater authoritativeness because her former student is on stage with her and is still suspicious of her.

Agatha does, however, momentarily risk revealing her vulnerability in the lines which give Mary hope:

'You and I,
My dear, may very likely meet again

In our wanderings in the neutral territory
Between two worlds.' (110-13)

What Agatha implies is that while Harry is elected to the
other world, Mary and Agatha have merely glimpsed the
messengers from that world; equally, their experiences of
frustrated human love have cut them off from the natural
world of relationships. There is a kind of limbo where they
wander, not by choice but by the tragic effect on their lives of
relationships that have not been fulfilled. It is a weary
comment, consistent with the tiredness Agatha has already
expressed to Harry: 'neutral' is safe but anaemic and
'wanderings' lack energetic commitment to life.

Perhaps Mary captures the mood of these lines and feels
that they come from some deeper experience in Agatha's life
than her former principal has ever dared reveal to her student.
Mary is, perhaps, over-generous to Agatha in then attributing
her new perspective to Agatha's wisdom in making her wait to
discover that Harry must go. It may also seem rather
unbalanced that Agatha reveals so little of herself to Mary and
yet elicits from her a total revelation of her feeling of
desolation to her harsh teacher with poignant gratitude. But it
is not untypical of Mary, a timid girl, to allow herself to be led.
Perhaps this helps the actress playing Mary to suggest that her
change of heart grows from the account she hears from
Agatha. The relationship between them remains very much
that of senior and junior, teacher and student.

What does life hold for Mary at the end of the play? Her
question about whether it is now too late to apply for a
fellowship is never answered because Amy bursts in with, 'So
you will all leave me!' (123). Presumably Agatha will help
Mary cope with her loss, but it won't be a very jolly life and we
can only hope that Mary's human warmth does not freeze as
Agatha's had done. The sombre tone of the chant of Agatha
and Mary at the end, as they pray for the curse to be ended,
may be contrasted with the explosion of joy of the Women of
Canterbury, transforming previous images of horror into
expressions of God's creative energy in the world. The spirit of
Easter informs the praise of the Canterbury women, a
penitential Good Friday awe hangs over the chant of Agatha
and Mary. While Harry looks towards his new life with a

certain amount of joy in following the bright angels, the final ritual only offers Mary and Agatha a hope for consolation for what has been lost.

Such a resolution cannot be summed up simply as Eliot rejecting human endeavour. Had things not gone so deeply awry; had not Agatha's deep love caused Amy such deep hurt, had her illicit love not required renunciation, human love might have been powerful enough to effect a reconciliation – as it does in *The Elder Statesman*. The quest of a religious solution in *The Family Reunion* is an acknowledgement of the tragic within humanity: it is not a denial of humanity itself. What Eliot has given us is a play in which the central character becomes convinced of a religious vocation that he must answer; the demand of his calling leaves other characters confused, heart-broken or silently wounded as his departure destroys their expectations. Eliot dramatises the human cost: there is Amy's bitter insight and death. Mary, who goes on living, is poignant because she bravely seeks to cope with a pain which she feels all the more sharply because of her generosity in human affection.

# 7

'Under Compulsion of What Experience . . . ?'

There is little doubt that *The Family Reunion* was intensely personal in its implications for Eliot, and two of the author's letters throw interesting light on this. On 6 April 1939, Eliot replied to the Bishop of Chichester, George Bell:

> Thank you very much for your kind letter. I quite accept your criticism of the play; indeed I saw fundamental flaws before I had finished – so fundamental that the only alternative to accepting them was to scrap the play. I could not find any way of projecting interior crisis into physical action. However, I am content to have got rid of what has been lying in my mind for some years, and hope that I may now proceed to something more object-ive.[1]

On one level this letter makes an apparently fair, objective criticism of the play, which prepares for Eliot's later more public dissatisfaction[2] with *The Family Reunion*. He diagnoses a dramatic deficiency: Harry's interior crisis is not translated into physical action. Certainly we have seen that Harry is a baffling character, one that we may not take to, one who is enigmatic to himself, his family and the audience. The crisis is interior and not given strong stage reality. The Furies, Greek imports in the English country drawing room, fail perhaps to be the necessary theatrical metaphor for the crisis. However, we have already argued that Part I successfully dramatises 'the awful privacy of the insane mind' by having Harry, afraid that he actually is mad, struggle for a coherent expression of his elusive emotion. In his scenes with Agatha there is, if not physical action, at least character interaction, which develops both our and Harry's understanding of his state of mind. In doing this, Eliot's method is consistent with the drama of the confessional duologue that we have been examining.

Even if it remains true that Harry's interior state is elusive in theatrical performance, the view of the play I have been putting forward can make a certain virtue out of the enigma. Any difficulty Eliot has in realising in terms of dramatic action the interior crisis of Harry assists the communication of the other drama, the tragedy of the rest of the family, whether uncomprehending, baffled, sad, hurt or rejected by Harry's strange illumination. Arguably, the harder Harry is to fathom the more our sympathies are balanced across the full range of characters, rather than residing exclusively in the spiritual hero.

Eliot's letter to Bell seems to be saying something beyond merely offering a critical insight into his sense of the play's artistic failure. 'I am content to have got rid of what has been lying in my mind for some years, and I hope that I may now proceed to something more objective'. Certainly, on the literary rather than personal plane, Eliot had been experimenting with smaller motifs in *Sweeney Agonistes* in 1923. There, too, had been the struggle of a haunted mind to put horror into words. But in Eliot's use of the word 'objective' there is a hint that the material he was handling was too personal for him; he could not be detached enough to give it an independent physical life in stage terms. There is perhaps a hint of catharsis in the fact that the play got written and it was better to go on to exorcise Eliot's own horrors than abandon the attempt.

The inseparability of an artistic failure and a too close personal entanglement with the experience may be pursued through a reference to his own criticism of *Hamlet*. A week earlier than his letter to Bishop Bell, Eliot wrote to a friend from Kelham, Brother George Every:

> I quite agree with the critic . . . who pointed out that my own criticism of the weakness of Hamlet, which I made many years ago, could be used against my own play. I regard this play, myself, merely as a necessary stage which I had to pass through before writing a satisfactorily

objectified drama.[3]

It was in the *Hamlet* essay that Eliot coined the phrase 'objective correlative'[4] and clearly in his use of 'objective' and 'objectify' in these two letters Eliot still regarded the points that he made in that essay as important. Translated into terms of Harry's problem, the Hamlet criticism would be that Harry is 'dominated by emotion which is inexpressible, because it is in excess of the facts as they appear'. The emotion he expresses does not arise inevitably from the situation and the chain of events enacted on stage. The interesting detail from our present point of view is that in the *Hamlet* essay Eliot indicates that Shakespeare's artistic problem arises because of a personal experience which befell and baffled Shakespeare himself. 'We are surely justified in attributing the play . . . to a period of crisis . . .'; 'the supposed identity of Hamlet with his author is genuine to this point: that Hamlet's bafflement at the absence of objective equivalent to his feelings is a prolongation of the bafflement of his creator in the face of his artistic problem'; ' . . . under compulsion of what experience (Shakespeare) attempted to express the inexpressibly horrible, we cannot ever know. We need a great many facts in his biography.'

We are given a salutary reminder by Peter Ackroyd that 'The game of "hunt the author" is a barren one'[5]. It is not the purpose here to establish one-to-one relationships between characters in *The Family Reunion* and Eliot's own family. Nonetheless the general pressure of the material is undoubted, and a brief exploration of this leads to a more subtle reflection: it reinforces our sense that the play reveals Eliot to be more human than his detractors give him credit for.

The letter to George Every suggests the personal rather than the professional nature of Eliot's difficulty with the play. It is hard simply to see *The Family Reunion* as a 'necessary stage' for Eliot the playwright to pass through before creating more objectified drama. The Plutocrat scene in *The Rock*[6] shows evidence of a dramatist able to handle ideas in a sufficiently objectified theatrical form; and his handling of the theme of martyrdom in *Murder in the Cathedral* reveals no such problems of objectivity. It must, therefore, be the material of the play which he finds intractable. As a stepping stone to further thoughts on the nature of Eliot's achievement in the play we should pause to outline some of the possible biographical influences which put pressure on the play.

One of the most sensitive analyses of Eliot's early years is the book[7] by Lyndall Gordon tracing the growth of his religious sensibilities, from his Unitarian New England childhood to his conversion to Anglicanism in 1927. The biographical elements are handled carefully, bringing in just so much as is necessary to fill out the spiritual autobiography which lies in both published and unpublished poems. It seeks to understand the nature of Eliot's religious experience and brings the reader into sympathy with aspects of his faith which at first sight have put people off – the emphasis on sin and purgation. It is written in the light of the recognition of how much of his poetry is born of the intense experience and searching of the author himself.

I have also found Peter Ackroyd's extremely readable biography[8] a particularly useful source for the material of this chapter. I am not intending to throw new light on Eliot's life, but to suggest that Eliot's life throws light on the nature of his achievement in *The Family Reunion*.

There are two particular moments prior to 1939 when Eliot submitted to the awful daring of a moment's surrender. Both involved a major turn-about causing pain to others although each was an essential stage in Eliot's own spiritual journey. The first was his marriage to Vivienne Haigh-Wood and his decision soon after that to settle in England rather than return to his family in America. This decision also involved disappointing his father by giving up his prospects at Harvard. Then, after a turmoil of a marriage for both Eliot and Vivienne, Eliot seemed to be seeking a second new start when he was confirmed into the Church of England and took on British nationality; at this time he had been thinking of leaving Vivienne. although the separation did not come until 1933. In 1938 (the year before *The Family Reunion* was completed) he would have been involved in some way in the decision to have her confined to the sanatorium at Northumberland House.

Such decisions were agonising. The marriage with Vivienne clashed with his sense of loyalty to his family and their

exacting standards and expectations. Although his decision to
marry involved apparent rejection of parental hopes for him,
he always had a strong sense of familial pride; 'in the little flat
in Crawford Street, Eliot kept a corner of family photographs
and silhouettes; he also wore an Eliot family ring'.[9] When his
father died in January 1919, he felt the acute regret of not
having yet had a chance to prove himself in his father's eyes.
Even the dissertation on the philosophy of F H Bradley, which
Eliot had promised his parents he would complete, and which
in 1916 was accepted by Harvard, had not turned the tide of
his father's disappointment. Eliot never travelled to take up
the doctorate they offered.[10] His father's death 'was a terrible
ordeal for him.' It robbed him of his chance of publishing a
book in America which would show that, by settling in
England, he had not 'squandered his life and talents'. Henry
Ware Eliot[11] 'had died without seeing any evidence of his son's
capacity except for a few strange poems in a slim
volume.'[12]

There were two family reunions in Eliot's own experience
that were full of the tensions between a decision which he felt
to be right for himself and the pain that he knew this caused
his parents. The first was when he travelled to America in July
1915 to inform them that he was married. The marriage had
been a precipitate affair. Lyndall Gordon[13] suggests that his
failure to take his parents into his confidence earlier may have
been to do with Vivienne's sexual attractiveness to the shy,
inhibited, studious Eliot: 'Eliot married quickly on the crest of
a moment of rapport, so abruptly that there was not time to
inform his family. It was almost necessary for Eliot to act
impulsively – to forestall habitual scruples – if he were to act at
all'. Eliot stayed in America for about three weeks before
returning to England; he never saw his father again and it was
six years before he met his mother again. Peter Ackroyd[14] has
suggested that Eliot was guiltily sensitive to this as an act of
'betrayal'. Although his father thought his son had taken a
wrong course, especially as Vivienne could not accept the
suggestion that they came to America so that Eliot could
continue his studies, he did not cut off the allowance he was
already giving his son. Nonetheless the dissatisfaction Henry
Ware Eliot felt with the marriage is reflected in his will
whereby he did not leave money outright to Tom as he had to

his other children: the inheritance in his case reverted to the Eliot family on Tom's death.[15]

Throughout this time Charlotte and her son remained fond of each other. Something of a poet herself, Charlotte's ambitions for her son had been literary. Eliot corresponded regularly from England, and he wrote an introduction to her verse drama *Savonarola*. From the time of Eliot's visit to America to tell his parents of his marriage, Charlotte began to worry much more about him, suffering from nervous anxiety at night.[16] She, like her husband, regarded highly the practical application of a person's abilities, and it may be that the desire not to disappoint in this respect made Eliot endure school-mastering before he transferred to Lloyd's bank and eventually Faber and Faber: 'It would have been unlikely for Eliot to make a precarious living, like many English writers, by freelance or part-time work. He had to prove himself to his father . . . (and) to recover the approval of his mother who had always scorned 'the man without a hoe'.[17]

The second family reunion was in 1921. He clearly longed to see his mother again, inviting her to England six years after his marriage. She was to come to him because he could not afford the fare to America, but he was worried that his seventy-seven-year-old mother would be very frail. In fact she turned out to be full of energy. It is suggested, however, that the visit was a strain on Eliot, precipitating his nervous illness later that year, because he needed to keep his marital problems out of sight, with Vivienne living quietly in the country.[18] After his mother had left, Eliot collapsed and went to a nerve specialist. There are about this visit and Eliot's breakdown signs of the tension of guilt; the marriage which he wanted but which caused pain to other loved ones. 'He had already written to his brother, in the previous year (1920), saying that he did not think he could ever be happy again until he could see his mother, the 'see' is underlined, as if to emphasize the physical proximity which he desired.'[19] He had not seen her since the previous delicate reunion in America, and in that time she had been widowed. Thus in the background of this new meeting was Eliot's unresolved conscience regarding the disappointment he had caused his father. Eliot was eager to have *The Waste Land* completed in time for his mother's visit[20] – perhaps as a sign of success within his chosen life of exile. He was also anxious that the failure of the marriage that had caused her pain should not impinge on her visit. He thought she would not wish to see Vivienne in any case feeling that she blamed his wife for his decision not to return to America. In fact they did meet, and it was Charlotte who provided for her in her will of 1923.[21]

What do these biographical details contribute to our understanding of Eliot's achievement in *The Family Reunion*? Certainly nothing as fruitless as giving easy equivalents between fact and fiction; Amy is not identifiable as Charlotte. Rather they help us to recognise pressures experienced by Eliot in his own life which become dramatised in characters in the play. Eliot thus knew the inner conflicts and tensions in relationships underlying family meetings after strained absence. The title of the play stresses the familial aspect of the drama, and the action has the unknown quantity of whether unresolved tensions in close relationships will reach a satisfactory conclusion, or produce further pain. The hero's marriage against parental wishes was known personally to Eliot, but the indications of his biographers show that he knew the pain he caused; he did not gloat in his rebellion but suffered acutely because of his knowledge that what he did disappointed others dear to him. It is my argument that Eliot's sensitivity in his own experience to the pain he caused others enables him to enter imaginatively into the emotions of Mary, Amy and Agatha. He does so at a level deeper than is realised by those, including at times Eliot himself, who schematise the play into characters of varying degrees of spiritual illumination. Further, in Eliot's own terrible ordeal of his father's death before he could satisfactorily resolve the disappointment he caused, lie the seeds of the experience when Harry leaves his mother without being able satisfactorily to heal their wounded relationship. Personal experience in Eliot's life becomes dramatised in the play as the 'tragedy of the mother', and the audience is able to feel the pain Harry causes. Harry himself may not understand what he is doing to the people around him; Eliot the playwright does, and in dramatising that insight he gives us a play very much more sharply objectified than Eliot the commentator seemed to realise.

These family tensions took place between 1914 and 1923

but left their impact. More frequently, commentators point to another personal crisis which puts pressure on *The Family Reunion* the tragic progress of the marriage itself, the destructive intensity of Tom and Vivienne's lives together, their breakdowns, his decision to be separated and her eventual committal to a mental home where she died.

Again Lyndall Gordon is sensitive in her discussion of this delicate area. Also, Peter Ackroyd's account of the desperate situation in the marriage which seemed to force Eliot into painful decisions is convincing. The separation finally came in 1933, although it was certainly in Eliot's mind back in 1925.[22] The parallels between the experience of Harry and the circumstances of the Eliot marriage hardly need stressing; the marriage which parents regretted and the son disappointing familial expectations; the unhappiness of the marriage leading to its break-up, in one case with a metaphorical death when Vivienne entered Northampton House, in the other with a drowning which Harry thinks makes him a murderer. It is all too credible that Harry's guilt at his wife's death reflects Eliot's feelings of guilt at his leaving Vivienne and subsequently, as a trustee of the Haigh-Wood estate, financing her stay in the mental home.[23]

While Peter Ackroyd warns against hypothetical identification of Harry's guilt with Eliot's separation from Vivienne, he does remind us that *The Family Reunion* was being written 'during the period which led to her committal in Northumberland House: "You would never imagine anyone could sink so quickly" is Harry's comment on the death by drowning of his wife. And the description of her – "A restless shivering painted shadow" – is very close to contemporary accounts of Vivienne herself.'[24] It is important to my reading of the play that the guilt experienced by Eliot is dramatised not simply in Harry's horrific pursual by the Furies and his search for his purifying destiny. It is dramatised in the family reaction where he portrays their pain. From reading Lyndall Gordon and Peter Ackroyd on the failure of Eliot's marriage it is clear that he knew that, in carrying out the decisions he felt to be inevitable, he would cause pain. Indeed, judged by other people, many aspects of Eliot's behaviour seemed harsh; Eliot's strategy for avoiding any meetings when Vivienne desperately tried to see him at Faber's after the separation is said to have caused her 'humiliation and anguish'.[25] Vivienne never saw the separation as inevitable, but once Eliot knew this to be the right course for him he seemed to need to be ruthless in carrying it out. Equally he felt doomed to execute his decision in a way that clashed with his sensitivity to the feelings of Vivienne. Ackroyd asserts that no-one in Vivienne's family criticised his decision to leave her at the time.[26] However, if Robert Sencourt[27] is reliable, Eliot was aware of the cruelty of his manner of separating. Ackroyd[28] relies on Sencourt when he writes: ' . . . when Maurice Haigh-Wood' (Vivienne's brother) 'asked Eliot if there were any other, less cruel, way than of writing through solicitors, he replied, "What other way *can* I find"?' Such a reply indicates a desperate man who knows he will cause pain.

Ackroyd's reflection on Eliot's words, 'What other way *can* I find?' is interesting: 'It is a difficult question to answer; the only alternative would have been a private confrontation, and of that both parties seem to have been incapable. He had followed what seemed to him the wisest and best course, by separating from his wife physically, while superintending her through the proxy of friends and relatives. . .'[29] There may be a cowardice in such action, leaving the dirty work to others. However, while Eliot could not personally minister to Vivienne, there seems little doubt that he genuinely cared for her welfare, even if others had to make the contact. In 1925, when he wrote to Russell about the alternatives to their marriage, he feared that Vivienne might not be able to manage to live on her own, although he does not complain in this letter of her illnesses.[30] While in America delivering lectures at Harvard in 1932 and planning the separation, he wanted to know how Vivienne was.[31] Eliot had taken religious counsel, and heeded the advice of friends over the years before 1933[32], and felt that Vivienne would be better without him, but anxiety remained about whether separation would worsen her nervous complaint. He also blamed himself in part for the damaging relationship: 'living with me has done her so much damage'[33]. Countering the criticism that Eliot was callous in using his secretary at Faber to stall Vivienne while he escaped from the  building, Anne Ridler, who also worked for Eliot in the situation, feels that no humiliation or anguish would in fact have been saved had the two met. She adds significantly that 'while Eliot himself found Vivienne's pursuit of him humiliating and agonising, he never felt indifference to her pain'.[34]

The picture that emerges is of a man who may not have been able to express his concern convincingly to the other person, but who found himself forced into a decision that was vital to his own being, who felt the decision was also essential to the other but feared its effect, and who, in carrying it through, appeared to lack sensitivity while inside he suffered, knowing the painful consequences of his choice and behaviour to the other. If such an assessment of Eliot's inner crisis is accurate, it makes the nature of his guilt more than is revealed through Harry alone in the play. Another dimension of that guilt gives a source within Eliot's experience for his empathy with the suffering of Mary, the tragedy of Amy, and the bafflement of other relatives.

Relating the marriage to the progress of Eliot's religious experience, Lyndall Gordon writes: 'His marriage was the grim underside of his life, the secret inferno to be traversed before he might be worthy of the genuine awakening only Christianity could supply.'[35] This is a central idea in *Eliot's Early Years*: the American Puritans saw themselves marching across a wilderness to create a new ideal for mankind. 'For Eliot's mother the wilderness was also charged with moral meaning. In *The Man Without the Hoe* Charlotte Eliot hails America as the place where pilgrims came, not out of greed, but to try themselves morally in a wilderness, to face 'the rocky shore' and 'a churlish climate'. This notion of pilgrimage from imperfection to perfection was deeply rooted in Eliot's family and their Puritan past. For him to experience the world as a waste land was a prerequisite to experiencing it in faith.'[36]

Such an observation seems crucial to our understanding of the final area of personal pressure in *The Family Reunion*. Harry finds that his choice of marrying and leaving Wishwood has only led to an unhappy relationship, compounded by guilty fears that his wife's death has fulfilled his wishes. The return to Wishwood cannot undo the consequences of that choice, and the supernatural agents pursue him until he interprets their message; he must leave the family home to find his freedom, and, as Agatha hopes, lift the curse of the family itself. The

imagery of the moral test in the desert comes in Harry's first
attempt to put his destiny into words:

> 'To the worship in the desert, the thirst and depriva-
> tion,
> A stony sanctuary and a primitive altar,
> The heat of the sun and the icy vigil . . .' (II ii 331-3)

Harry's destiny takes him away to a life described in images
akin to those Lyndall Gordon cites for the testing in the
wilderness as part of the progress to perfection. Such a
progress seems to have been Eliot's as well in his baptism and
confirmation into the Church of England in 1927. Again here
was a vital decision in Eliot's life which baffled and hurt
people around him by the manner in which he announced it
to the world[37] and the secrecy in which the ceremonies were
performed.[38] It appears that in some ways his Christianity was
a solace in the midst of desperate personal circumstances.
Also the privacy of the ceremony, without even his wife there,
suggests an intense need for a private relationship with God
outside of his marriage.[39] One aspect of Eliot's attachment to
Anglicanism is described by Lyndall Gordon as 'a means of
support and self-correction'.[40]

We have seen that Harry's destiny to follow the bright
angels requires leaving behind human relationships for a
personal testing and purifying in some kind of wilderness. It
shares something of the penitential nature of Eliot's own
embracing of Anglo-Catholicism. Eliot described his
admission to the church as beginning a long journey afoot[41],
and he was irritated with those who felt he had just settled into
an easy chair. It is important to consider alongside Harry's
destiny in *The Family Reunion* the contrasting affirmation of
human ties and love which is the theme of *The Elder Statesman*.
It is significant that, even in *The Family Reunion*, where the
religious dimension is austere, even vengeful at first, Eliot has
been able to dramatise the human cost in the reactions of
other characters in the play. The humanity is there which
later, in days that were happier personally for Eliot, emerges
in the plot of *The Elder Statesman*.

It is possible that the guilt in Harry which seems to exceed
the objective circumstances of the play relates to Eliot's own

crises. It derives from his sense of having failed the high hopes of his father and of having abandoned his family; of his part in the misery of his first marriage of which both his mother and father disapproved; and of his responsibility for his separation from Vivienne and his approval of her being confined in Northumberland House. We can argue two ways from this; we could concur with Eliot that the pressure of personal material undermines the artistic objectivity of the finished play; or we could claim that the fact that the underlying emotions within the character of Harry were akin to those Eliot had experienced gives the play an authenticity, an urgency and passionate commitment that the later plays lack, with a corresponding diminishing of their hold on the feelings of the audience. The protective wit of *The Cocktail Party*, and the neatness of the scheme of things in *The Confidential Clerk* make the plays in the end less warm in human terms than the cold house of *The Family Reunion*.

# 8

---

## A Matter of Form and Performance

Cutting into the relationships of the human beings in the play are the Furies. Like the goddesses in the 'Oresteia', these figures begin as the Erinyes and end as the Eumenides, 'the bright angels'. Their presence in *The Family Reunion* has irritated people because they are imported Grecian deities who have no place in the drawing-room of English landed gentry in the 1930s: rather than assisting Eliot to communicate a view of life where supernatural and natural worlds interact, the clash of styles makes the supernatural world border on the comic.

Raymond Williams has studied the problem in Eliot's convention of mixing supernatural with natural speech in character with speech in chorus, and differing intensities of poetry. I shall refer several times in this chapter to what he has said. His argument must be taken seriously in any attempt to defend the play's success in performance, for he has pinpointed major problems and expressed his criticism succinctly. To his *Drama in Performance* I am grateful for opening my eyes some years ago to critical methods of treating literary text as script for the theatre. He outlines Eliot's problem: 'The interest and difficulty of *The Family Reunion* is that the action takes place on at least two levels; the physical reunion and its declared relationships, which are directly written; the spiritual encounter, and its undeclared but revealed relationships. The complexity of the play is in the consequent relations between these two planes of action, and thus this is at once a problem of meaning and a problem of drama in performance'.[1] It becomes clear that Williams regards the spiritual action as the one that really mattered to

Eliot, and that the choice of the naturalistic setting crippled his serious dramatic action.[2] It will be realised that this is where my conviction about the play differs from Williams's. If the dramatic action that Eliot has succeeded most in presenting is the tension between a divinely authenticated experience that takes Harry away and the human hurt that such a destiny causes those who are left, then the relationship between the two levels of the play's convention may after all have dramatic integrity.

In *Drama in Performance* Williams illustrates the problems more closely by looking at details from certain scenes. First he examines the dilemma of the Furies essential to the action, needing to be seen, but contradictory to the whole naturalistic setting of the play. Then he tackles the chorus of Uncles and Aunts: the physical realism of the stage scenery makes dramatically impossible the images by which the chorus expresses its fear of surprises: different landscapes seen through the same window, stairs up taking you down, going out through a door and finding yourself back in the same room. Finally he moves to discuss the co-existence of two types of verse: in one the stresses follow the meaning in a single tone; in other lines, belonging to character parts, the stresses cannot be made to relate to the same scansion without 'measured gravity', where the tricks of conversational rhythm are required. In *Drama from Ibsen to Eliot* Williams refers to a Martin Browne production where the Uncles and Aunts shift from consciously played dialogue to formal speech; this confirmed his feeling that such transitions were unplayable[3]. The reference to this production is omitted in the later revision of William's book, but he does retain the belief that the relatives are comic characters, and he thus finds it incongruous when they are required to adopt a formal commentary.[4]

The tone of Eliot's verse is discussed more fully in Williams's revision, *Drama from Ibsen to Brecht*. He identifies as a permanent method of Eliot's 'The imitation and repetition of commonplace speech, and then its contrast with intensity'.[5] Such a method is well suited to Eliot's purpose because it is a form 'designed to express the interpenetration of different levels of reality'.[6] He argues that it is at its most successful when the change of level is 'not consciously pointed by the author'.[7] Often, however, Eliot betrays his lack of confidence in his convention by drawing attention to the contrasts. I shall argue that where abrupt changes occur in the level of the verse there is often a dramatic, as opposed to an apologetic, point being made.

## I THE EUMENIDES

I shall begin the discussion of these formal points with the Eumenides. Since these are a theatrical, not a literary problem, the discussion in this chapter will focus on their staging. They will be justified, if at all, in performance, not in academic debate. A producer cannot, in the end, sit on the fence; he has to make decisions which are tested in performance; alternative ideas have to wait until a new production can be mounted. It appears that only recently have convincing ways of presenting the Furies been found. It was Michael Elliott's production that finally won over the play's first producer, E Martin Browne, who had come to think the Furies unstageable, save in the imagination.

Productions of the play and experiments with the Furies disappointed Eliot in that he never saw those 'ill-fated figures' work in performance. By 1951 he is able to see humour in the situation:

> 'They must in future, be omitted from the cast, and be understood to be visible only to certain of my characters, and not to the audience. We tried every possible manner of presenting them. We put them on the stage, and they looked like uninvited guests strayed in from a fancy dress ball. We concealed them behind gauze, and they suggested a still out of a Walt Disney film. We made them dimmer, and they looked like shrubbery, just outside the window. I have seen other expedients tried; I have seen them signalling from across the garden, or swarming on to the stage like a football team, and they are never right. They never succeed in being either Greek goddesses or modern spooks.'[8]

Eliot saw the absurdity as his failure to 'adjust the

ancient with the modern'.[9] While this is in part true, the
theatrical practitioner E Martin Browne sees the awkwardness
extending into the stage setting and directions: the upstage
'window embrasure' where the Furies appear makes it
impossible for Harry to see them and register his reaction
facially to the audience – this upstaging of the actor
undermines key moments in the development of the part.[10]
Raymond Williams has gone further still to argue that it is not
the clash of Greek and modern which makes the Furies
absurd, but the clash of the supernatural with the
naturalistic.[11]

## a) Classical and Modern

The first of these difficulties can be seen in details of the
setting and costuming of the original production at the
Westminster Theatre. Here Martin Browne stressed in various
ways the Greek connection, and thus may have needlessly
added to difficulties in reconciling the ancient with the
modern. Eliot came to regret this emphasis:

> 'I think now that it was a mistake to draw attention to the
> Greek element, both by the use of the term Eumenides
> and in the notice which Martin Browne wrote for the
> programme; because it seems to have worked merely to
> draw the more intelligent critics off on a false start.'[12]

The set further highlighted Greek echoes, with the window
embrasure suggesting a portico of a classical temple. The
drapery across the window itself suggested the sweep and
hang of Grecian robes. It dominated the centre of the back
wall, like a further proscenium arch in which decisive actions
were to be played. The pedestal for the Grecian-shaped vase
holding the late flowers of Wishwood also had a classical line
tapering towards the base.[13]
The producer, Martin Browne, had time for second
thoughts when, after five weeks, the first production was
interrupted by war. He was dissatisfied with the set and asked
the original costume designer, Stella Mary Pearce, to create a
new house for the much smaller stage of the Mercury Theatre

in 1946. Here the challenge was to create the essential feeling of a large house on a tiny stage. Browne described the new set being skilfully extended over the proscenium arch[14] by painting it to match the door and window-frames of the room.[15] Stella Pearce explained that her intention was to build one corner of a large L-shaped room, the more intimate part used for the informal family gatherings.[16] The implication of further space reaching out into the auditorium in no way suggests airiness. In contrast to the rather bright impression and clean lines of the Westminster set, the walls were dark. Faint yellow and white streaks gave the only sheen in the otherwise sombre atmosphere. In place of Grecian suggestions, the feeling now was neo-classical but with a Victorian heaviness. An eighteenth-century bust – very much the treasure of an English country-seat – occupied one angle of the room and gave a sense of scale, as did the large central window. Reviewers praised the adaptation of the scene to the small stage,[17] and in solving this practical problem Stella Pearce created the oppressiveness of the house so essential to Harry's revulsion on his homecoming.

What this new setting shows is that for the play's revival the classical references were lessened and more attention was given to the atmosphere of the play. It is this progress towards creating a self-sufficient theatrical impact, without reliance on the allusions to Aeschylus, which contributes to the success of later productions of the play.

In designing the appearance of the Furies, Stella Pearce experienced the difficulty of the classical heritage in the country drawing-room. Eliot's scenario pictures 'one man and two women, in evening dress'. The first draft sees them as the Eumenides who 'appear in the window embrasure', but Eliot writes in 'Evening Dress', opting for black tie.[18] Stella Pearce believes that her own copy (now untraced after being sold through an agent to America)[19] described 'three young men with suitcases'. This would have related to Harry's predicament as a voyager. It is interesting that Martin Browne cites the modern-dress Furies as an example of Eliot's original conception failing to adjust the ancient and contemporary[20], whereas Stella Pearce wished that Browne had not persuaded Eliot in favour of a more classical portrayal.[21] She made models dressed in wool jersey of the same style as that worn by the actresses. The simple dresses were dyed so that Amy, Agatha and Mary were in different colours, and this scheme was echoed in the clothing of the Furies, linking them to the three women who have most influence over Harry. This human form, however, was made deliberately ambiguous by the models having bird-mask faces with beaks and the hands were claws. Stella Pearce felt that such an allusion to the bird-like nature of the mythological Furies would be missed by many of the audience. If the Greek significance of the bird features were lost the figures looked comic.[22]

Later, in a northern production of the play, Martin Browne and Stella Pearce experimented with lighting to create the supernatural presences. Three small glass prisms on invisible threads descended and, revolving a little, caught special lights in a rather eerie way.[23] Once again, therefore, we see the staging problems presented by Eliot's 'ill-fated figures' being tackled by aiming to create atmosphere rather than underlining their classical parentage.

The idea of the Furies being three young men, or even a man and two women in evening dress would have suggested that the supernatural beings were in fact extensions of Harry (the whole family change for dinner), or of people who were part of Harry's crisis. By eventually settling on the term Eumenides, for all its difficulties, Eliot does achieve a degree of autonomy for them. They clearly become agents beyond Harry, and their influence on him during the action of the play is seen to be more than a projection of himself, or a personal fantasy.

We move, of course, here towards Raymond Williams's objection that it is incongruous in the physical realism of the play to portray agents from the spiritual world. To this we shall come. First, having considered the appearance of the Furies in Martin Browne's production in connection with the classical source, we need to look at the other physical problem they create in staging the actors' movements and reactions.

## b) Visible or Invisible?

Martin Browne discusses the awkward implications of the stage setting and directions. The script reads 'The curtains part, revealing the Eumenides in the window embrasure'[24], and this creates immense logistical problems in the blocking of Harry's moves as he reacts to his ghosts:

> 'In order to show the Eumenides in the window embrasure, the director must place the window in the back wall of the set. This means that, in each act, Harry must be facing upstage, with his face away from the audience. This is a grave mistake; and Eliot is right in saying that none of the devices that either he or I have used or seen others use has overcome this handicap. The Eumenides, whatever they look like, however eerie the sounds or lighting effects which accompany them, cannot involve the audience in an experience which cannot be seen upon the face of the character who alone can mediate it.'[25]

It is perhaps strange that Browne had not foreseen this problem in the first draft of the play; if he did discuss the practical implications of the stage direction with Eliot he does not recall it in his book on making the plays. Browne says that Michael Redgrave was handicapped by the positioning of the Eumenides upstage at the moment in Part II when he had to communicate his fresh understanding of their nature.[26] Redgrave himself saw the Furies, which impinge on Harry's consciousness the very moment he enters the room, as creating a monumental task for the actor:

> 'I was required to enter into the drawing-room of Wishwood . . . where my family were assembled, not having seen them for eight years, and immediately be transfixed with fear at the sight of the Furies, who have pursued me.'[27]

The problem of the Furies is also the problem of the actor who is haunted by them:

> 'Only once, late in rehearsal, did I manage to get this extraordinarily difficult entrance right, to convey the fear and the suffering which are necessary without being merely melodramatic.'[28]

It is indeed a tough assignment; Amy assumes that John or Arthur has arrived; she is amazed that it is Harry who comes in much earlier than expected. She exclaims and in the crowded room, 'Harry stops suddenly at the door and stares at the window.'[29] We have to remember that the window is upstage, and so the strength of the entry of this major character is weakened by his having to look away from the audience before the actor has even had time to establish himself on stage. The Uncles and Aunts then offer brief words of welcome before Charles spots something is wrong, and Amy rebukes Harry for indecorum because he has closed the curtains himself. The Furies are not visible to anyone on stage, nor to the audience at this point. They are in Harry's imagination. He knows how he has just seen the family as he passed outside the window, and defends himself with: 'Do you like to be stared at by eyes through a window'.

Eventually Martin Browne came to agree with Eliot that in future the Eumenides must be omitted from the cast and be understood to be visible only to certain of the characters:

> 'Accordingly, the last time I did the play, I set it as follows: the window, in the stage left wall, the door in the right. Both are classical in design and are strong features balancing each other.
>
> When the Eumenides appear in Part I, they are only seen by Harry through the window: we see nothing except a change of lighting, and Mary who is looking at Harry does not see them when he does. She does, of course, see them (as she later reveals to Agatha); but only at the moment when she makes the supreme effort of drawing the curtains across and denying their existence.
>
> In Part II, Harry and Agatha both see them at once in the window. At
>
> > 'I know that you are ready.
> > Ready to leave Wishwood, and I am going with you.'
> >
> > (II ii 234-5)
>
> both characters see them moving through the room between actors and audience. When Harry says
> > 'No! you were already here before I arrived.'

they are downstage centre. They then move towards the door and go out of it, leaving Harry, who follows them, at the door at the end of his speech. Agatha has been upstage of him during the Eumenides' progress. She delivers her 'rune', not in the window embrasure but upstage centre, looking at Harry as 'my child, my curse'. When she breaks the spell with
'What have I been saying?'
he comes away from the door.

This plan lets us see the Eumenides, not in visible shapes but through the imagination of the actors, and allows to the actor playing Harry the full opportunity of registering the change wrought in him by their appearance and of responding to their summons.[30]

There are interesting groupings suggested here, but this is something of an 'air-drawn dagger' solution. What is interesting is that the producer who worked closest to Eliot is prepared to alter Eliot's own stage directions and to use effects of lighting. Such a departure from the printed script may be justified in that Eliot himself suggested the invisibility idea. In the 'after-life' of a play each production needs to seek the most effective way for its time of communicating the play; the concept of its staging may lead to alteration in the original stage directions, or they may be enhanced by different resources of the theatre. This will be an important consideration when we come to consider what Michael Elliott did with the Furies.

However, making the Furies invisible to the audience does not seem a satisfactory solution. Simply, it is irritating to an audience anxious that they may have missed something important. The prisms referred to by Stella Pearce were satisfactory in this respect because they caught the eye – there really was something there to be seen. On other grounds, too, Eliot was really evading the issues when he suggested invisibility, because to make the Furies insubstantial raises questions about their reality. Admittedly we are told that the chauffeur and Mary have seen the 'ghosts', and we see Agatha respond to their presence when they become 'the bright angels', but it is unsatisfactory for an audience, not seeing them, to have to take their manifestations on trust from the actors' facial expressions. Furthermore, if all the appearances of the Eumenides have to be invisible, the production loses the important distinction between Harry's fear that they are peering at him through the open curtains on his arrival, and the later occasions when they actually are here to be seen by Mary and Agatha as well. This distinction is part of a theatrically effective building-up of tension – at first we do not see anything and, like the rest of the family, are amazed, even alarmed, by Harry's eccentricity and we fear for his sanity. Later we realise there is something real causing Harry's nightmare, then further questions as to the nature of these beings occupy our interest until their next appearance as bright angels. Once again it is important to the play that, although Harry's departure is painful to others on the human level, we are to know that his need to leave Wishwood is a genuine destiny and not falsely inspired by hallucination. If we are able to see their manifestations we do not feel that we're the dupes of clever mediums up there on stage. As we argued earlier, they cannot just be visual counterparts to Harry or the women who have influenced him, for this reduces belief in their autonomous existence as supernatural beings. We have to be challenged to consider that the supernatural realm is real.

## c) Spiritual Revelation

Before we turn to how subsequent productions have tried to make the supernatural credible within the physical medium of the stage, we need to clarify the nature of the spiritual revelation which makes the presence of the Furies essential to the play.

We saw that if Harry is not trapped in the 'awful privacy of the insane mind' the spectres must have an existence separate from him, and that this has implications for their staging. He had thought that his frustration with his wife, wishing her dead, had led to his pushing her overboard. Thus phantoms haunt him to punish him, and he goes home in the hope of throwing them off. He is alarmed that he senses their presence all the more acutely at home. He doubts his own sanity. Ironically, Mary's pretence that she cannot see them reinforces his sense of lunatic isolation. Because, however, the audience has seen them we have evidence of their authenticity. In Part II, with enormous relief when Agatha and he see the Furies together, Harry accepts the reality of the spectres. They are more than projections of an hallucinating mind. The question is, what do they now reveal to him, other than that he is not mad?

We have seen that part of his coming to accept the objectivity of the Furies is that Agatha has explained the family secrets: the origin of his unhappiness is dated before his birth. Properly understood, his misery does not originate in his failed marriage. So far, any revelation has come through conversation with Agatha on the naturalistic level. It has prepared the way for Harry's accepting that the Furies do not have a vendetta against him. The spiritual significance of the supernatural presences is then a matter of interpretation, and Agatha begins this; she hopes that he will be the one to take on the tragedy of the family and go through purgatory on their behalf, not least atoning for her own guilty part in the unhappy past. To Harry, the nature of their revelation is initially much less exalted. The 'spiritual' guides are to be trusted because their uncompromising pursuit of him drove him to discover why it was at Wishwood, of all places, that they haunted him most: he has now understood that his personal freedom from the inhibitions of the past lies in leaving the source of that unhappiness behind. In this way they may be seen as *providential* – a power beyond the natural order of things cuts into a family reunion to indicate that Harry's destiny lies elsewhere. This is the extent of the revelation. They, unspeaking, never tell him what he must do but only insist, by the strength of their presence, that remaining at Wishwood is inappropriate for him. What he tells Amy leads her to think he is going to become a missionary.[31] But he has only talked vaguely of what he will do in images drawn from that desert imagery of the test of worthiness we discussed in the previous chapter. 'Worship in the desert', 'thirst and deprivation', 'stony sanctuary and primitive altar', 'icy vigil'.[32] There is a missionary hint in 'care over lives of humble people', but the emphasis is more on a personal and testing discipline. We can see why he feels this is necessary to him from earlier lines to Agatha alone; he feels 'befouled' by his experience of marriage and what he learns of the family tragedy; he needs to purify himself, trusting that this will open the way to reconciliation.[33] It is an austere decision on his part and, in so far as it is a Christian interpretation of the Furies' presence, it is on the ascetic, rigorous side of the faith, involving service to humbler folk but containing only a little hint of some future renewal in human reconciliation. We have seen that the fact that Harry has an alternative life leaves others behind, sad, confused or heart-broken; in the previous chapter we linked this with pressures in Eliot's own life towards a sublimation of unhappy human relationship into a penitential journey to God.

In so far as the signals of Providence are Christian ones, therefore, they contain only part of Christianity. Commenting on the towering figures of the Royal Exchange production in the 1970s, Katharine Worth felt the fundamental ambiguity of the Furies had been given effective theatrical presentation: 'black and malign to view in the first shock of their appearance, yet perhaps to be seen differently, as soaring, upward-pointing beings. The question remained open: the movement toward an orthodox Christian solution at the end was not strong enough to obliterate the disturbing impression made by the strong physical impact of these Eumenides.'[34]

Others have not found dramatically effective ambiguity. Michel St Denis, reassuring Redgrave that the difficulties in the play were not of the actor's making, felt that there was a failure of imagination on Eliot's part in not making it clear where Harry and the Chauffeur were to go.[35] Once again Redgrave had found the Furies baffling, and in order to play Harry he felt he needed a clearer idea of where they actually go at the end.

'I had wrestled with this question in rehearsal for some days before daring to broach it to Eliot himself. 'Well,' he said, 'I think they would probably go off and find jobs in the East End.' They might, but from the tone of his reply it was apparent that he wasn't at all sure.' (*In My Mind's Eye* p 141).

Although Redgrave found this answer inconclusive it does suggest that missionary work in the desert may not be the only interpretation of what Harry's duty is to be. Martin Browne says that Eliot would not want to make the future of Harry too precise in a play 'which was meant to retain, at least in respect of its central theme, a universal and timeless quality'.[36] Perhaps here we see the producer's commitment to religious ideas in the play leading him also to be less than practical in helping the actor get to grips with the part. An actor needs detail if he is to focus his performance, particularly if, like Redgrave[37], he finds Stanislavsky's method of approaching a part through particulars to be the most helpful.*

However, what is powerfully imagined by Eliot is that the Eumenides are agents of Providence, warning Harry away from becoming master of Wishwood: his mother's wish would continue to stifle him. This 'message' of the Furies is in tune with what we witness on the natural level of the characters in action during the play. There is no inconsistency here between what we learn on the spiritual and the natural levels.

I stress the point that the alternatives open to Harry are a matter of interpretation by him and by Agatha. Harry's treatment of his mother, tragically unable to let her into any understanding of his experience, is not required by providence; treating his mother hard is the only way by which Harry at this stage in his progress is able to handle the human situation. Furthermore, while Eliot may be wanting to suggest a more universal dimension to Harry's destiny, and while this may lead to his failure in imagining the particulars necessary for the actor to play Harry, he has succeeded in giving us a more credible person in his chief character. Harry is still young in understanding his new direction, and is unclear what it will mean in practical terms, apart from the necessity of leaving home. He fails to communicate properly with his mother at their farewell partly because he does not yet fully grasp what he is to do. It might be in a line of reasoning such as this that an actor finds a way of making the call to an unknown destiny plausible to himself and then to the audience.

---

* May 1937 (2 years before playing Harry) Redgrave bought copy of *An Actor Prepares*. Became a disciple of Stanislavsky and subsequently took advice for a proposed production of *Uncle Vanya* from Stanislavsky's widow.

## d) Supernatural and Natural

Raymond Williams agrees that the play demands the figures of the Furies to establish the non-human dramatic reality[38]; their objective character is the means of transformation from Harry's sense of being pursued to his sense of following 'bright angels'. But Williams also sees that behind the difficulty of presentation is a problem of dramatic imagination and dramatic writing: how to graft 'a play of spiritual revelation on to the most enclosed of all theatrical forms, that of the fixed, entering and exiting, country house group'.[39] 'The difficulty, one might say, in *The Family Reunion* is not the Furies but the "window embrasure" and its stage-set drawing-room and library. It is the scenic establishment, in the dramatic conception of the play, of a kind of reality, the fully furnished country house with which not only the Furies, but the whole inner conception and theme, are incompatible. This cannot be solved by excising the Furies.[40]'

Williams has written elsewhere that he read the play before he saw Martin Browne's production of it. He found that the uncertainty of convention which he felt to be in the text was 'deepened and emphasized on the stage'.[41] He admits to having no idea how the Eumenides might convincingly be made to appear, 'but in the performance which I saw I became suddenly aware, beyond the window embrasure, of a constellation of green headlamps, or signal lights. I am prepared to do without Aeschylus' snakes, and I am aware of the diversity of all such manifestations; but this oddly glowing cluster beyond the curtains seemed to me a little short of adequacy.'

What is of particular interest here is that, despite the difficulty in Browne's production, Williams implies that performance might be able to resolve the problems of clashing conventions. By looking at developments in more recent productions I hope to suggest that there is a theatrical potential in the Furies which, when realised on stage, seems to override the objection that they contravene the conventions of the drawing-room realistic drama; the supernatural assumes a terrifying force for the audience as well as Harry.

There were certainly those who felt that Peter Brook in his 1956 production had coped successfully with the hitherto unsolved problem of how to present the Furies. Brook prepared for their coming by gently darkening the stage and the Furies were bat-like apparitions on the scale of a Henry Moore sculpture.[42] *The Times* urged that 'There is no straining of the imagination to suppose them either Greek Goddesses or modern spooks'.[43] J C Trewin gives a vivid account of the presentation:

> '. . . the shapes are seen beyond the tall windows of Wishwood. The lights fade; fire-glow pulses round the room, filled now with curving, wave-like shadow. The curtains slip back, and outside the window are dimly visible the pursuing shapes – in any form in which we like to picture them. We are aware of their presence; each onlooker must define them as he wishes. Later in the play, before Harry knows he must "follow the bright angels", light glimmers where all has been grey, as though a moon is shining serenely over the estate and touching the tall dim forms with silver. Peter Brook has let our imaginations take charge. We see what we want to see. It would be wrong to be more explicit, and Brook is not a director to misjudge an effect . . . what stays with me most is atmosphere, not text.'[44]

What J C Trewin shows is that *The Family Reunion* has theatrical impact which the Furies heighten if they are treated using the resources of stage lighting; the intensification of the fire-glow in a darkening room is an ominous stage image; the fluid wave-like patterns of the fire-light across the walls of the country house diminish their appearance of solidity and make plausible the visitation of less substantial figures, massive yet spiritual; the lyrical, almost romantic transformation in the lighting for their final appearance when the Furies become positive angels of brightness provides the audience too with a reassurance of beauty in the bright angels. Thus the naturalistic world is transformed so that the admission of the supernatural is not incongruous. The atmosphere does not, it seems, require the actor's face to communicate the experience to the audience. This, perhaps was something that Martin Browne might have stressed more: if the whole stage picture before our eyes becomes part of the experience, the apparitions communicate directly to us without our needing Harry's visible reaction to mediate their impact. What is happening in Peter Brook's production is that the Furies become bolder because they are handled more confidently. Rather than the Furies being a trifle apologetic for turning up outside the window, their presence affects the whole stage: in terms of theatrical communication they really do transform the reality of what we see on stage. We do not need to seek out the *Oresteia* in programme notes, we do not need to supply their *raison d'être* intellectually, nor do we find them embarrassingly grafted onto a drawing-room play; they are allowed to hit us in the senses and generate emotional response in us as well as Harry. This is at the heart of theatre; it has its own language for communicating to an audience which is different from that of the printed text. The successful production finds the appropriate theatrical metaphor for the idea the text contains.

It is precisely this finding of an appropriate metaphor in the staging to convey the interweaving of the spiritual and the physical that made Michael Elliott's various productions[45] of *The Family Reunion* stand out for making the text work in the theatre. His theatre in Manchester was 'in-the-round' and his conception of the play, which translated to the Round House and ultimately went into a run on the proscenium stage of the Vaudeville, was determined by the fact that the audience would be wrapped round the action. Thus the set was not itself a solid three-dimensional structure, but a skeletal room with realistic furniture in the centre of the theatre. Suddenly problems disappear, and new opportunities for communicating the play's themes open up. First, the conventions of in-the-round staging, by now well established even for naturalistic drama, permit rooms to be indicated without the full realism of reconstructed walls. It therefore becomes easier to transcend the physical nature of the setting and allow other dimensions of reality to flow in and out. Also the house was no longer the solid oppressive building of some earlier productions but a skeletal affair through which the audience looked to see the action of the play and, of course, the audience on the other side[46]. Immediately the theatrical situation emphasizes the notion of the audience as watchers in a special way not possible in the proscenium theatre. It is also inevitable in in-the-round productions that the actors and actresses come onto the stage through the audience; this link with the audience can become a significant feature of a production. Edward Fox's first entry as Harry in Michael Elliott's production gained in power because as he moved in through the audience he paused 'with them for a long look at the family exposed to view a few yards away in the lighted framework before stepping into it and exchanging the watcher's role for the actor's.'[47] This gives Harry a chance to establish himself before he makes his official entry into the room to stare at the window, that crammed moment that Redgrave found so difficult to bring off.

Having shared Harry's perspective of the family from outside, the audience finds more forceful the irony of Harry's ridicule.

'How can you sit in this blaze of light for all the world to
look at?
If you knew how you looked, when I saw you through the
window!
Do you like to be stared at by eyes through a window?'
(I i 222–4)

Such a staging immediately links the audience with eyes that are looking through a window on the house. This gives a more sinister twist to our previous amusement, when Eliot played with a metaphor from theatre to express the uneasiness of the Uncles and Aunts summoned at Amy's command to a reunion none of them particularly relishes.

'Why do we feel embarrassed, impatient, fretful, ill at
ease,
Assembled like amateur actors who have not been
assigned their parts?
Like amateur actors in a dream when the curtain rises, to
find themselves dressed for a different play, or having
rehearsed the wrong parts,
Waiting for the rustling in the stalls, the titter in the dress
circle, the laughter and catcalls in the gallery?' (I i 203-6)

Katharine Worth who was in the audience analyses the

theatrical justness of the effect of Harry's paused entry through the audience:

'By this simple arrangement, an experience which can seem private and obscure in the far distances of the picture-frame stage was brought nearer and made comprehensible.'[48] 'Elliott was able to involve us in uneasy complicity with Harry's point of view; we too spied on the oblivious family, understood, as they could not, his neurotic consciousness of being watched; were threatened when the scene darkened and the monstrous shapes descended between us and the interior giving enormous urgency to Harry's attempt to evade them.'[49]

She describes further the added benefit of this staging when it came to the Furies:

'Michael Elliott successfully disregarded Eliot's injunction against making the Furies visible, contriving, with the aid of beautifully controlled modulations of light into darkness, spectacular incarnations from them as towering black shapes, alarmingly materialising between the audience, who sat round a skeletal framework enclosing the haunted room, and the character. . . .The physical involvement of the audience in Harry's experience was completed when the Eumenides materialised between him and them, overlooking both, forcing them out of their safe role as watchers into the protagonist's situation of vulnerability to the inquisitorial eye. In appearance, these Furies were essentially shapeless bundles of old clothes which might or might not contain life. They conveyed the fundamental ambiguity of Eliot's Furies, black and malign to view in the first shock of their appearance, yet perhaps to be seen differently, as soaring, upward-pointing beings.'[50]

It is a tribute to Michael Elliott's staging of the play that Martin Browne hailed it as combining rounded character-isation 'with a presentation of the Eumenides which gave equal (and terrifying) validity to the "nether world".'[51] It was, he felt, a definitive production of Eliot's greatest play.

This production moved to a proscenium theatre for a longer London run after the Round House, and it was felt by members of the cast to be artistically less successful on the more orthodox stage. Certainly the transfer to the Vaudeville lost some of the insights given by performance in the round, the powerful involvement of the audience in the play's ambiguities of watchers and watched, for instance, and the nature of a skeletal set which could without severe jolt be the venue for supernatural agents. Nonetheless the Furies were terrifyingly introduced. When Harry enters from backstage and is instantly afraid of his pursuers, the stage darkened with three pools of downlight in a semicircle round the drawing-room. When Mary and Harry see the Furies, the identical places are taken by the towering figures, impossible to make out in detail in the dim room. When they appear to Harry and Agatha there is a flash as of lightning across the white figures so bright that the audience is momentarily blinded; when the normal lighting is restored the audience is not quite sure what it saw, but knows it has witnessed a revelation. The revelation of 'bright angels' was quite different here from the serene moonlight effect described by Trewin in 1956. It was stark and uncompromising, momentary, leaving the characters on stage to interpret its meaning. For each intimation and sighting of the Furies, the expertise of the lighting designer startled our eyes with an other-worldly intersection of the contrasting logic of cause and effect in the dialogue of the characters. The production made us believe that the action was never far from an eerie world ready to challenge assumptions in the normal patterns of life. Rather like the successfully sustained ghost story, the production established a method – largely through dynamic use of lighting changes and levels – for hinting that supernatural influences lurked just out of sight throughout the action, not just at the key moments when the presences are at their most focused.

## II THE CHORUS

The charge of inconsistency in Eliot's style has been applied also to his treatment of the Uncles and Aunts. Here again, Eliot lost faith in what he had done. 'For one thing, the immediate transition from individual, characterised part to membership of a chorus is asking too much of the actors: it is a very difficult transition to accomplish'.[51a] An approach to a solution lies in how the overall staging assists the actors in their task. It also lies in appreciating how the choral passages

actually relate to their normal conversation, and here
Raymond Williams presents doubts about the mixture of
styles in a powerful case that needs answering.

*The Guardian's* praise of the staging of the Furies at the
Vaudeville extends to the boldness with which the Uncles and
Aunts change from speaking as individuals to chorus.
'Elliott's production accepts the play's abrupt transitions . . .
and never tries to disguise the changes. . . . Huge white
shrouded Ku Klux Klan figures emerge to stand in a vengeful
circle around him. His aunt's description of the dangerous
hot summer when she saved his father from committing wife
murder is organised in a darkened room, a single spotlight
held above her. The use of lighting and spotlight to arrange
for formal choric speeches accomplish the shift away from the
real world of motor accidents and dressing for dinner.'[52] Once
again in performance the play seems best served by treating
the contrasts of style head on. The Uncles and Aunts must not
apologise for their transitions; the audience needs to be
conscious of the abrupt changes. Well tackled, these
transitions become part of the process whereby the audience
is made deliberately uneasy, and the feeling that processes
beyond the logic of natural cause and effect are at work within
this eerie country house. The process in this case is that of the
subconscious mind demanding expression. Once again,
lighting and grouping provide the key.

Again, Raymond Williams found his uncertainties about
the text confirmed when he saw the Uncles and Aunts in
performance in a Martin Browne production.[53] Because the
dialogue between the Uncles and Aunts had been consciously
played with characteristic 'flicks and starts' of ordinary
speech, the movement to the required degree of formality for
the chorus seemed quite impossible. An apologetic manner
resulted: 'The aunts and uncles stepped into a self-conscious,
rather solemn line, turned up their eyes and recited.' Where
the Vaudeville production, which I saw differed vitally from
the staging recalled here by Raymond Williams, was that
when the Uncles and Aunts slipped into Chorus they did not
always regroup themselves. The transition was marked by the
actors assuming a stiller and more formal bearing; a change in
the texture of lighting signalled a momentary drop into their
collective unconscious. In their choral speaking we could

believe we were being allowed to hear what mental activity was going on below the level of their conscious thought. They seemed not to lose their characters but to be revealing to us more of their true nature and situation.

My previous analysis of the Uncles and Aunts is crucial to making the transition in the level of their speech dramatically acceptable. It is here that we are able to question Raymond Williams. His reading of the text, reinforced presumably by the presentation he'd seen on stage, led him to see the Uncles and Aunts on the naturalistic level as deliberately comic in their characterisation.[54] While I agree that they are comic, I have argued that the humour is not just light entertainment, but is woven into the dramatic irony of their situation at Wishwood. They fear ridicule, but their behaviour is at times ridiculous because they are forced by Amy's stage management of Harry's reception to fall into stereotyped social roles. Their predicament is intensified by the fact that the Uncles and the Aunts represent different sides of the family, sides which meet rarely, are quite different in their social expectations and who have to get on somehow with one another because Amy has brought them together. Harry's return after a failed marriage and bereavement causes family embarrassment.

Raymond Williams bases his dissatisfaction on the 'formal convention' which 'depended on a sudden change of function by the Aunts and Uncles, who had been set in a deliberate comic characterisation and were required suddenly to become agents of a formal commentary; this was not easy to accept.'[55] If this is what was happening, it would not be easy to accept. My argument suggests that it is an oversimplification to see them as being set in a 'deliberate comic characterisation'. Similarly, I do not think that they change 'function'; they change level – they go from the awkward conversation where their exposed weaknesses are amusing, to a subconscious level where they reveal that they know they are vulnerable and feel confused faced with Amy's scorn and Harry's extraordinary behaviour. Rather than becoming 'agents of a formal commentary', the chorus explains and gives depth to their roles as individuals in the social interaction. In performance this change in level can be reinforced by the use of lighting so that we witness a visual as well as verbal change.

The convention of reaching to words and attitudes below the surface is found elsewhere in drama. The naturalism of O'Neill's *Desire Under the Elms* is broken at one stage where the son and the father's new wife express their as yet unspoken passion for each other by being seen in their respective rooms, looking as if through the partition wall at each other and drawn irresistibly together. *The Caucasian Chalk Circle* which requires realism in demonstrating the hunger of a man on the run, also allows a singer to describe the thoughts of two lovers tragically unable to communicate their feelings to each other. At their first meeting the dialogue of the lovers is sustained at a highly formal level in a play which also has realism of dialogue for the malingering peasant. It may be objected that Brechtian techniques work towards a different, more polemical and detached purpose than Eliot's. However, Chekhov, with whose dramaturgy we have already compared some of the processes in *The Family Reunion*, offers a further instance of formal grouping and choric style to bring out the collective thoughts of characters previously conceived naturalistically. *The Three Sisters* ends in such a way, with the band playing cheerfully as the soldiers leave the three women bereft of their hopes; Olga asks why there should be all this suffering, and she hopes for some happy issue. Her style is momentarily lifted beyond character as she speaks on behalf of her sisters assembled in a closely grouped vignette. It is my contention that to restrict a play to either a naturalistic or a formalised convention is to limit the way theatre may legitimately communicate.

## III VERSE

Much of the foregoing discussion depends for its consistency or its failure on Eliot's verse. Here again there is criticism, not least from Eliot himself, that the verse betrays the author's lack of confidence in two realms of the play's action: the literal and the poetically heightened. One of the reasons Eliot found his play to be  defective was 'the introduction of passages which called too much attention to themselves as poetry and could not be dramatically justified.'[56] He has in mind the device of two 'lyrical duets' which are isolated from the rest of the dialogue by being written in shorter two-stressed lines. Because 'beyond character', 'the speakers have to be presented as falling into a kind of trance-like state in order to speak them.' Furthermore, 'the member of the audience, if he enjoys this sort of thing, is putting up with a suspension of the action in order to enjoy a poetic fantasia'. Glancing at Shakespeare Eliot is depressed, for in Shakespeare a 'purely poetic line or passage . . . in some mysterious way supports both action and character'. We may, however, remind ourselves here of my previous discussion of the aria passages in their dramatic context though, of course, this is not to equate *The Family Reunion* with *Macbeth* or *Othello*.

We have seen how Harry's two lyrical duets are prepared for in the texture of the verse (Ch 2). Just before the duet with Mary, their dialogue had reached a point where Mary had achieved for Harry a momentary respite from his mental anguish. We saw how the rhythm and imagery had become more tranquil. We have also seen that the aria is dramatically justified as signalling the apparent success of Mary with Harry; yet we saw that this closeness contains their different understandings of their image of spring; Mary's hopefulness is set against Harry's horror and talk of blood. Thus the passage, far from being a poetic fantasia remote from the necessity of the action, is a passage of heightened language containing within it the seeds of the difference of emotion which is about to force the couple apart. The aria also gives a shape to the performance equivalent to Harry's image of a silence between two storms.

Similarly (Ch 5) we saw that the closeness implied by Harry's duet with Agatha concludes a two-way process whereby each has needed the other to lift his or her personal burden; Harry has needed Agatha's disclosures about the past; Agatha has needed to unlock years of guilty silence. Dramatically the duet is justified, sealing the relationship between them. Their respective images here sum up the lives they each have lived till this time, the hell of their phantom selves. The rose-garden image replaces the hellish, to symbolise their release into a loving relationship after the frustration of driving their capacity for gentler feelings underground: dramatically, this lyrical oasis prepares for

Harry's ability to accept the Furies as 'bright angels'. Thus again, Eliot's distrust of his play may be seen as needlessly harsh. The question that remains concerning the aria passages is how successfully they can be managed in performance. Once again Michael Elliott's production showed how the 'trance-like, inhuman effect often seen in performance'[57] could be avoided. Katharine Worth describes the way the production achieved a touching moment of human contact. In the arias the characters moved towards each other 'as the verse mounted to its climax. The embrace in which they met, sexless, yet touched with sexual tenderness, delicately suggested a real human communion at some deep level of being.' I, too, felt such an impression in the later revival of this production at the Vaudeville. The significance of tender physical contact is to establish the humanity of characters in a play which presents so much in the way of blocked human responses. I have noticed that producers of Eliot are sometimes shy of making his characters touch. For instance, in the production of *The Elder Statesman* at the Birmingham Repertory Theatre in 1979, the final scene of reconciliation, understanding and forgiveness between father, daughter and son-in-law was staged with the characters standing or sitting apart from one another. The text demanded physical closeness and contact, but sometimes a curious reverence for the Poet Eliot gets in the way of finding the necessary stage expression of the feelings that the lines convey. It is no argument to say that the lines convey it without the action endorsing the relationship between characters in view of the audience. Theatre must incarnate the ideas; gesture is necessary to maintain the humanity of the creations in performance. The coming together in an embrace of characters in the arias reinforces in visual detail the dramatic integrity of the text itself.

Another part of Eliot's dissatisfaction with the arias came from his concern in *The Family Reunion* with its versification. He speaks of trying to find a rhythm 'close to contemporary speech, in which the stresses could be made to come wherever we would naturally put them, in uttering the particular phrase on the particular occasion'.[58]

He then specifies the versification which he devised to answer his requirements: 'a line of varying length and varying number of syllables, with a caesura and three stresses . . . the only rule being that there must be one stress on one side of the caesura and two on the other'. He claims he worked this out for *The Family Reunion* and that this is substantially what he has continued to employ in the later plays. It is because the aria passages so clearly break away from the pattern by having only two stresses per line that they draw attention to themselves and betray his avowed aim of capturing the rhythm close to contemporary speech.

So far in this discussion I have taken the 'lyrical duets' to refer to Harry's moments of poetic intensity with Mary and Agatha respectively. Certainly Martin Browne identifies these as the passages that Eliot had in mind.[59] They are indeed the only obvious matched pair of lyrical moments that may be termed duets. They do not, however, have the two stresses per line that Eliot speaks of in relation to these passages. Rather they are a tightening of the play's characteristic line of three or four stresses, thus giving the effect of being more intense and, perhaps shorter. The only heightened poetry shared between two speakers which does tend towards the two-stress line is that of Agatha and Mary in the play's final ritual, round the birthday cake. In two, possibly three places, Agatha has what might be termed solos which have the two-stress feel to them; her 'rune' spoken in the window embrasure after Harry has seen and accepted the Bright Angels[60]; her cryptic conclusion to Part I,[61] and some of the lines in her mysterious images just before the first choric passage of the Uncles and Aunts.[62] The last two of these might certainly be felt to be out of character, and their poetry does draw attention to itself. Personally I find them the least satisfactory moments in the play, for it is on these passages that Agatha's claim to quasi-priestess status may be based. This status is not consistent with the unravelling of her character in the dialogues on the naturalistic level of the play. The lines have a wisdom to them, but are indeed the voice of a poetic commentator rather than the character Agatha. When the Uncles and Aunts speak in Chorus they are not beyond character, but they are going deeper within character consistently with what we see of their situation on the literal plane of the action.

In an earlier version of his essay *Poetry and Drama* Eliot is less specific about the versification, but seems to imply that it is the choric style speech that offended him, rather than the passages between Mary and Harry, Agatha and Harry. In 1949, in *The Aims of Poetic Drama*, he said that in *The Family Reunion* his chief preoccupation was 'to work out a form of verse as close as possible to modern conversation, and a form in which the most commonplace necessary remarks can be made without sounding absurd, and in which the most poetical language can be employed without its seeming affected.'[63] He claims only to have made 'some progress' in this direction. I would agree entirely with this earlier assessment. He goes on to say that he replaced the formal chorus, (Women of Canterbury), with choral passages spoken by one or more of the actors who take part in the ordinary dialogue and who also have individual parts in the play. Eliot confesses that while he still likes some of these choral passages 'as poetry', he felt the poetry was a 'little too obvious'; 'some passages were like an aria in Italian opera, where the action is halted in order that the audience may enjoy a lyrical interlude'. He admits to employing undramatic poetic props. The drama itself depended too much on the literary association with Aeschylus. He was going, in *The Cocktail Party*, to avoid poetry for poetry's sake.

I have referred to Eliot's 1949 comments not just because they are more relaxed, less masochistic in self-assessment than his 1951 version. Certainly his analysis is looser, but in a curious way it seems possibly more accurate than his later, more detailed comments. First of all, he does not see the need to pin-point the offending moments; he simply allows that there is still a tendency for him to write poetically, despite the aim of a more conversational rhythm capable of being sharpened when intensity is needed. He also does not specify the nature of the stress pattern in either the ordinary dialogue or the lyrical passages. This is important, for in *Poetry and Drama* which came after *The Cocktail Party*, he seems to me to have read back into *The Family Reunion* a progress in the versification which applies much more accurately to *The Cocktail Party*. It is very rare in the dialogue of *The Family Reunion* to find the line with three stresses regulated around the caesura; the four-stress line dominates. Occasionally there are three stresses in some passages, but these lines tend to come in the more lyrical passages alongside occasional two-stresses.

We can see this in a passage quoted by Raymond Williams[64] in which he argues it is relatively easy to discern the caesura and three-stress principle:

> If you want to know why I never leave Wishwood
> That is the reason. I keep Wishwood alive
> To keep the family alive, to keep them together,
> To keep me alive, and I live to keep them.
> You none of you understand how old you are
> And death will come to you as a mild surprise.
> A momentary shudder in a vacant room' (I i 82-8)

The only line here where three stresses naturally follow the meaning is:
'You none of you understand how old you are'. But even this line feels as if it is a deliberate variation of the more typical four-stress line:

> If you want to know why I never leave Wishwood
>
> That is the reason. I keep Wishwood alive
>
> To keep the family alive, to keep them together,
>
> To keep me alive, and I live to keep them.
> You none of you understand how old you are
>
> And death will come to you as a mild surprise,
>
> A momentary shudder in a vacant room.

Of course, this scansion is a crude instrument for catching the voice speaking these lines. For instance, a change of stress to the word 'I' rather than 'live' is possible in the fourth line to reinforce the emphasis on Amy. Also, pause and inflections all contribute to the rhythm heard in the theatre. My point is that it would be a curious delivery that actually made these three-stressed lines. One possibility might be:

> If you want to know / why I never leave Wishwood

That is the reason, / I keep Wishwood alive

To keep the family alive, / to keep them together,

To keep me alive, / and I live to keep them.

You none of you understand / how old you are

And death will come to you / as a mild surprise,

A momentary shudder / in a vacant room.

On the grounds that 'keep' is self-stressing by virtue of its being repeated it might be possible to attempt a scansion like the above which would have the effect of stressing only the words that might be highlighted in conversation, the forward movement of the key idea tripping over less significant words which might have received some emphasis in a more self-assertive verse form. This, however, is not what Sybil Thorndyke does in delivering the speech on a record directed in 1965 by Howard Sackler.[65] She treats it , as any actress naturally would, by not fitting it to rules but letting the logic of the rhythm of the words themselves take the lead. Sybil Thorndyke had watched her sister closely as she rehearsed the part of Violet with Martin Browne in 1946, and knew the play well.[66] As Amy under Peter Brook, Dame Sybil felt ill at ease: to her, Martin Browne had understood the spiritual music and haunting quality of the play more clearly.[67] With such a close affinity with the earliest productions and recording the play under yet another director in conditions where the voice carries the whole play, we might expect her delivery to be trusted.

I stress this at some length because Raymond Williams, relying on Eliot's specification for the verse form, uses this passage in comparison with the earlier words of Charles about civilised persons needing a glass of dry sherry or two before dinner.[68] He rightly says that the Uncles' speech does not scan in Eliot's new way, and suggests that this indicates the author's uncertainty of style; the uncle's lines need a lighter rhythm, in tune with the overall characterisation. My point is that Amy's speech does not naturally fit the Eliot scansion either. Rather,

Eliot's achievement is to have found a basic four-stress line, which as a skilful writer he is able to give more sonorous, or more colloquial stress as suits the situation and character.

That the three-stress line is more characteristic of *The Cocktail Party* than of *The Family Reunion* can be seen from representative passages from the later play:

Well, / I tried to do something about it.

That was why / I took so much trouble

To have those Thursdays, / to give you the chance

Of talking to intellectual people . . . (I iii 311-4)

or

/ You wished to be a hostess

For whom my career / would be a support.

Well, I tried to be accommodating. / But, in future,

I shall behave, I assure you, / very differently (I iii 336-9)

or

But even if I find my way / out of the forest

I shall be left / with the inconsolable memory

Of the treasure / I went into the forest to find

And never found / and which was not there

And perhaps is not anywhere? / But if not anywhere,

Why do I feel guilty / at not having found it? (II 613-8)

I am not claiming that these notations indicate the only way of delivering these lines. Indeed it would even be possible to give them a four-stress feel, and many lines in the play clearly do have four stresses. Rather I hope merely to point out how many sets of lines in this play may be given a conversational feeling by going for three key words in the line. The verse goes much more naturally into this scansion than do lines from *The Family Reunion*. The dialogue between Edward and Lavinia in the first two examples has the lively pace of a row whereby the voice skips over lighter stresses and pounces on key words that urge the point home. Celia's more reflective questioning in the third passage is at a more intense pitch poetically, reinforced by imagery, but the manner of delivery is still that of conversation with Reilly. Eileen Atkins, whose favourite speech as Celia is the one quoted above, has said of the verse in this play that it must be delivered naturalistically. Otherwise there is a very real danger of its sounding too 'holy'.[69]

Another reason for challenging the accuracy of Eliot's own assessment of the stage he had reached in developing his versification by 1939 is that *The Family Reunion* is much closer to ideas Eliot had about *Murder in the Cathedral* than it is to *The Cocktail Party*. *The Cocktail Party* is a wholly different form of play. It has no supernatural presences interacting with the human drama and, with the exception of the prayers for Celia, Edward and Lavinia, there are no clashes between realistic and formal styles and events. It is a play suited to the new form, which would be capable of bearing the rhythms and phrases of ordinary, colloquial speech, but which could be tightened up for moments of particular intensity or insight without the audience being aware of a jolt. Indeed we are not, as Eliot hoped, even aware of hearing verse at all.[70] However, Eliot's purpose in *The Family Reunion* demands and usually gets verse that fits his earlier, almost contradictory requirements. Four years earlier, at the time of writing *Murder in the Cathedral*, he was thinking that poetic drama must emphasise, not minimise, the fact that it is written in verse.[71] It needs to remind the audience that they are in a theatre and that they are hearing verse. This was because he felt that the tendency towards realism in the theatre had reduced the timeless nature of what the audience witnessed. Even the prose of such drama had been diluted to 'human noises'. The essential quality of verse is that it runs through the main action and offers a musical pattern 'which intensifies our excitement by reinforcing it with feeling from a deeper, less articulate level.' *The Family Reunion* is in many ways a transition play between the liturgical elements of *Murder in the Cathedral* and a more settled and consistent realistic method in *The Cocktail Party* ten years later. We have seen that *The Family Reunion* has bold contrasts that jolt the audience and that successful productions tend to be those which face this head on, possibly even risking the charge of theatricality from some reviewers.[72] The changes in the levels of verse need to be treated with similar courage. As a poet Eliot worked by contrasts, short descriptions, situations in one style of verse juxtaposed with very different types of passage and rhythm or a discursive paragraph. In *Murder in the Cathedral* he deliberately jolts the audience with the knights' speeches in prose and I believe in *The Family Reunion* he is still out to create strange juxtapositions in order to question the exclusiveness of any one view of reality.

Eliot's principal reason for using verse rather than prose as a stage convention for ordinary speech is described in *On Poetry and Poets*. 'It seems to me that beyond the nameable, classifiable emotions and motives of our conscious life when directed towards action – the part of life which prose drama is wholly adequate to express – there is a fringe of indefinite extent, of feeling which we can only detect, so to speak, out of the corner of the eye and can never completely focus; of feeling of which we are only aware in a kind of temporary detachment from action . . . This peculiar range of sensibility can be expressed by dramatic poetry, at its moment of greatest intensity. At such moments, we touch the border of those feelings which only music can express.'[73] This time, Eliot's comment on feelings which we can only detect out of the corner of the eye seems most appropriate to the dramatic experience of *The Family Reunion*. Because of this the poetry is rightly at the forefront of this play where it is not in the later plays.

I hope that the earlier chapters of this book have contributed to an appreciation of the integrity of verse as a vehicle for dramatic communication. Where necessary I have discussed the verse as a vehicle for dramatic speech responsive to and expressive of characters' moods, inter-

actions and situations. On the level of familial interaction I
have pointed to changes in Mary's speech from a formal,
protective style to a personal and vulnerable quality. We saw
the verse responsive to her testing the ground before trusting
others with her inner thoughts. We saw Agatha's sibylline
utterances in sustained, grammatical units within the verse
structure, and discussed her use of academic, cold discourse,
seeing it as another protective device before the broken
rhythms of lines where she prepares to reveal the truth to
Harry. We saw Amy breaking the flow of a line to insert a
pointed use of Agatha's name at a moment where the friction
between the two women surfaces. In the sections on Harry,
my analysis of his language was designed to show Eliot
handling it as a dramatic device to help actor and audience
understand movements of his tension; his fear of madness, his
difficulty in communicating to others what he urgently needs
to say, the tragedy of not finally breaking through to a new
understanding with his mother. Equally his language and its
rhythms revealed moments of relaxation and freshness and
hope. In this way the verse assists in giving us some focus for
the state of mind. We also argued that the verse becomes more
rhetorical at times when a character sees himself or herself in a
dramatic light: this applies to Amy as well as Harry. We have
also seen how Harry's two lyrical duets, which go below the
level of conscious thought, are prepared for in the texture of
the verse which precedes them. The choric speech of the
Uncles and Aunts draws attention to the stifling effect the
situation is having on their own unconscious feeling.

This analysis may go some way to allay the uneasiness
Raymond Williams imparts when he finds Eliot drawing
attention to changes in the level of the verse.[74] He is happiest
when the transition of level is not consciously pointed by the
author, as in the following:

'Gerald:    That reminds me, Amy
            When do the boys arrive?
 Amy:       I do not want the clock to stop in the dark,
            If you want to know why I never leave
                                            Wishwood
            That is the reason. I keep Wishwood alive

To  keep  the  family  alive,  to  keep  them
                                together,
To keep me alive, and I live to keep them.
You  none  of  you  understand  how  old  you
                                        are
And death will come to you as a mild
                                surprise,
A momentary shudder in a vacant room.
Only Agatha seems to discover some meaning
                                in death
Which I cannot find.
– I am only certain of Arthur and John.
Arthur in London, John in Leicestershire;
They  should  both  be  here  in  good  time  for
                                dinner.

                                        (I i 79-93)

Raymond  Williams  is  quite  correct  in  finding  the
deepening of the level with Amy's first line after Gerald's
question.  The  later  transition  back  to  business  is  also
smoothly achieved. But even here I wonder if Eliot is not
doing more with his verse. Something of the shifts in level of
the verse ought to be conveyed by the actress and sensed by
the audience, for they carry a significant point in the drama of
the relationships between Amy and her relatives. For Amy
there is not quite such a deepening of the level when she
begins her speech as quotation out of context might imply.
She has been lamenting that Mary did not marry Harry and
hopes that 'life may still go right'.[75] She attempts to drop the
subject 'Meanwhile let us drop the subject. The less said the
better'. This causes Gerald to go on to more banal questions
about domestic arrangements. However, Amy cannot yet
leave the implications of her plans for Harry and drops into
the poetic line, 'I do not want the clock to stop in the dark', to
sum up her fear of Wishwood being without a new master. She
talked then of death more explicitly; as we have seen earlier
her references to death unsettle the Uncles and Aunts who are
picked on here, and a resentful barb is shot in the direction of
Agatha, whom Amy singles out. That her preoccupation with
the bleakness of death is intended to disturb her relatives is

clear from the fact that she deliberately withholds her answer to Gerald's practical question for the duration of her disconcerting lines. Yet it was she who encouraged such a question by her previous line. With this addition to Williams's acknowledgement of the quality of this passage, I concur that the control of the verse reflects Eliot's confidence in his medium.

Certainly Eliot handles transitions in levels less subtly elsewhere. Williams cites Gerald's response to Agatha:[76]

> 'Agatha:  When the loop in time comes – and it does not
> come for everybody –
> The hidden is revealed and the spectres show
> themselves.
> Gerald:  I don't in the least know what you are talking
> about.
> You seem to be wanting to give us all the
> hump.' (I i 134-7)

Such a play for laughter here, typical of other responses of the Uncles and Aunts to more rarified speeches, seems to be part of Eliot's dramatic timidity. He is uncertain whether the audience will accept his convention whereby the different levels of verse are juxtaposed. He needs to reassure the audience with a comic return to normality, and in so doing undermines the really serious action of his play. What happens, Williams argues, is this: 'The level of experience, and so the character of the language, has gone beyond the tone of established probability. But then instead of contrast – the dramatic contrast of kinds of experience – the mixing of levels is regarded as uneasy, and is manipulated, negotiated, by a self-conscious – a falsely self-conscious – uneasiness.' 'The interpenetration of levels is most successful when Eliot is confident of his convention, and offers no explanation.'[77]

Yes, Gerald's line may well get a laugh; it may also irritate those who see the relatives as shallow people out of their depth in Eliot's spiritual scheme of things. But for all its obviousness, even awkwardness, it may be seen to have a dramatic justness in the context and the interplay of characters. Agatha we have felt to be a prickly character, prone to make cryptic comments, beyond other people's compre-

hension. We have also seen that Eliot questions this apparent
superiority in the scene with Mary where Agatha is allowed to
be unsympathetic. We have also seen Amy keeping Agatha in
check by edged comments. Indeed, before Agatha's speech
which prompts Gerald's remark, Amy has just tried to put
Agatha in her place. Agatha has talked of Harry finding a new
Wishwood, and that adaptation will be hard. This statement
contravenes all Amy stands for. 'Nothing is changed, Agatha,
at Wishwood'.[78] Amy's next lines amplify this consistency in
the nature of Wishwood. Agatha does not deny that
Wishwood itself is unchanged. but says that Harry, with all his
subsequent experiences, will have to encounter his old self
and all that might have been. Gerald, feeling that putting
Agatha down is the order of the day from the impresario of the
reunion brings in his own brand of dismissing Agatha's
insights. He says Agatha's conversation is not cheerful for
Amy's birthday, thus,[79] apparently trying to gain credit with
Amy. It appears that his alliance with Amy in the rivalry
between the two sisters is rewarded:

'Thank you Gerald. Though Agatha means
As a rule, a good deal more than she cares to betray,
I am bound to say that I agree with you.' (I i 143-5)

Thus even a cruder drawing attention to shifts in levels of
language can have a contribution to the interplay of
relationships within the drama of the family reunion. Much
more is going on in his verse than Eliot seemed to recognize
when looking back on his achievement. It is not just a matter
of how many syllables there are in the lines. Eliot had more
assurance than seems to be recognized about what work he
could make his verse do in terms of the drama.

Eliot's description of the new verse form he was devising
suggests that he was aiming for greater naturalism: 'the
stresses could be made to come wherever we should naturally
put them, in uttering the particular phrase on the particular
occasion'.[80] A naturalistic conception of dramatic action is 'the
kind of thing this character might, in all probability, be doing
at this point.'[81] He required such a form if he was to compete
on the commercial stage, by offering a vision of ordinary life
susceptible to spiritual interaction. There are, of course,

limitations to all forms of stage realism. The idea of poetic drama being naturalistic is something of a contradiction. The characters would not be likely to utter verse in any real circumstances. Eliot makes sense of this by distinguishing between prose, verse and ordinary speech. Thus prose on stage is as artificial as verse, or alternatively, 'verse can be as natural as prose'.[82] In choosing verse rather than prose to render contemporary speech, Eliot believed a dramatist could more readily express those aspects of 'feeling which we can only detect . . . out of the corner of the eye and can never completely focus.' In adopting verse, therefore, Eliot acknowledges that he will want to take his drama at times beyond the realistic surface of ordinary life. Thus his form, while it can handle some aspects of experience on a naturalistic plane, enables him to move to what is going on within men and women, and also to introduce influence from beyond the logic of time and space.

## IV CONCLUSION

I have referred to the naturalistic level of *The Family Reunion* several times, and on two counts. First, the setting of the play is a physical representation of the living-room and a library. Second, I have been arguing that the portrayal of the way members of the family relate to one another is conceived with psychological realism. The characters are most vivid theatrically when the actresses and actors can find motivations and understanding living in a rich subtext just beneath the surface of their dialogue. This quality of characterisation shares something with Ibsen and something with Chekhov. In most cases the inner action of the characters is eventually revealed in scenes of intimacy between two people and thus revelation here is consistent with the naturalistic character-'isation. The developments happen as they may reasonably be expected to in the course of real life. The exception is the Uncles and Aunts, whose inner feelings are deliberately suppressed by the situation on the naturalistic level of the family. For them, Eliot exploits a device which is more expressionistic. In so doing he also recognizes, as all theatre must, that there is a limit to the kind of experiences that can be revealed through recreating the probability of day-to-day relationships.

The Furies, we have seen, present a direct challenge to that daily logic of cause and effect, and they have to be given theatrical presence to establish their authenticity; the most successful presentations seem to have been the ones that openly acknowledge that they are intrusions on the naturalistic interactions and the material nature of the setting. The physical reality of the rooms at Wishwood has been variously presented. The first production stressed the classical allusions. The post-war revival conveyed the oppressiveness of the house, thus giving a 'scenic metaphor'[83] for Amy's view of life from which Harry must escape if he is not to be stifled. So even at their most realistic, the sets have had symbolic implications. The fluid effects of the lighting in Brook's production enabled the solidity of the walls to be questioned in anticipation of the Furies. The in-the-round convention of Elliott's production enabled physical reality to be conveyed in the furnishings but the skeletal framework, suggesting the boundaries of the room, made plausible the intersection of the spiritual. In other words, production needs to accept that the play is not fully naturalistic if it is not to be embarrassed by the supernatural. It succeeds when it acknowledges that the play trembles between the two dimensions.

Michael Elliott said in a programme note to his production: 'The reason why it has often been passed over as just another relic of the theatrical poetic revival before and after the war is that is does not explicitly treat the ordinary world as convincingly as the extraordinary.'[84] He admits to being obsessed by plays in which two worlds co-exist on stage – one realistic, the other entirely unsubstantial and yet at least as real. In *The Family Reunion* he felt that it needs 'on one level to be brought gently but firmly to earth – as an English Chekhov – so that on another level it can fly. Otherwise it bumps, bumps on the runway like a crippled bird, and never takes off. Only by being very real in one world can it make the other appear . . .' It was his presentation, not only of the airborne level but also of the family dialogue on the earth, which convinced me of the power of this play in the theatre. He seemed to me to succeed in keeping the relationships between members of the family extremely human, and the ingredients from the unconscious and from beyond were staged so that they compelled us to reckon with these as other kinds of reality: not alternative realities, but forces that make demands on the more familiar world of rooms where families meet. He showed me that the play worked, to use Eliot's terms, in giving us 'the human drama, related to the divine drama, but not the same.'[85] The goal of this book has been to explore the area often missed by literary critics, the creation of the human drama, the level that needs in production to be brought gently but firmly to earth. I hope that I may have shown that Eliot was a playwright of a very high order in his creation of the family, and in dramatising their tensions, and not least of all their suffering. True to his belief in a divine drama, Eliot uses non-naturalistic devices to present other kinds of reality. These devices, which may appear to contradict the naturalistic elements of the human drama, can in performance be made so theatrically vivid that both worlds are made convincing to the spectator. The core of the drama is not the salvation of the son nor the tragedy of the mother, but the various tragedies of mother and family and Mary in the face of the destiny signalled to Harry by the spiritual powers.

I hope also that the foregoing chapters provide a reinter-pretation of the play convincing enough to counteract Eliot's sense of defeat in failing to objectify Harry's state of mind and his illumination. If initially Eliot thought he was writing exclusively about a hero with a mission of salvation the play refuses to fit the mould; sometimes, even while writing, Eliot realised that the rest of the family suffered, and that the play was also tragic. In 1961 he seemed to think that if it was Amy's tragedy then it wasn't the salvation of the son, and therefore the play failed. What he could not entertain, in his public statements at least, was that what the play dramatises is, in fact, this very ambiguity. My biographical analysis suggests a reason why Eliot's play may have got closer to the truth than his critical statements about it – from what we learn of Eliot's own choices in life, he himself suffered because he knew that decisions he had to make for himself caused pain to his family and to his first wife. It is this double awareness that I feel lies at the heart of the power of the play. Rather than being a single-minded play with Harry as saint-hero, there is a human tussle between his affections and his calling. The drama lies in a genuine conflict between the two. One person's necessary choice causing pain to others is something Eliot understood, and the artist in him triumphs over the analyst. This contrast between the artist and the critic in Eliot accounts also, I suspect, for his ruthless comments on Mary as a distraction from Harry's true calling, and yet, at the same time, for his increasing creative sympathy with Mary through the drafts of the play.

# BIBLIOGRAPHY

The books listed below are those referred to in the preceding text. In the notes which follow references are to the name of the author; where more than one book by the same author is cited the reference is followed by the initials of the title. All line references to the text of *The Family Reunion* are to the Faber Educational Edition, edited by Nevill Coghill.

## I WORKS OF TS ELIOT

ELIOT TS   *The Rock,* Faber 1934.

ELIOT TS   *The Family Reunion,* Ed Nevill Coghill, Faber Educational 1969.

ELIOT TS   *The Cocktail Party,* Ed Nevill Coghill, Faber Educational 1974.

ELIOT TS   'Rhetoric and Poetic Drama', 1919 in *Selected Essays,* Faber 1951.

ELIOT TS   'Hamlet and His Problems', 1919 in *The Sacred Wood,* 1920. Reprinted in *Selected Essays,* Faber 1951.

ELIOT TS   Introduction to *Savonarola* by C Eliot, London 1926.

ELIOT TS   *For Launcelot Andrewes,* Faber 1928.

ELIOT TS   'Dialogue on Dramatic Poetry', 1928 in

*Selected Essays*, Faber 1951.

ELIOT TS     'The Need for Poetic Drama', THE LISTENER XVI, 25 Nov 1936.

ELIOT TS     'Religious Drama: Medieval and Modern', UNIVERSITY OF EDINBURGH JOURNAL, Edinburgh & London IX i (Autumn 1937).

ELIOT TS     'The Aims of Poetic Drama' ADAM XVII 200, Nov 1949.

ELIOT TS     'Poetry and Drama' 1951 in *On Poetry and Poets,* Faber 1957.

ELIOT TS     'The Three Voices of Poetry', 1953 in *On Poetry and Poets,* Faber 1957.

## II  CRITICISM

BROWNE EM     *The Making of TS Eliot's Plays,* Cambridge 1969.

DONOGHUE D     *The Third Voice: Modern British and American Verse Drama,* Princeton University Press, 1959.

GASKELL R     *Drama and Reality: the European Theatre since Ibsen,* Routledge and Kegan Paul, 1972.

HARRIS WM     *Theatrical Style and the Work of TS Eliot,* (Doctoral dissertation.) D.A. (37) 3988 A, 1976.

JONES DE     *The Plays of TS Eliot,* Routledge & Kegan Paul, 1960.

KENNEDY A     *Six Dramatists in Search of a Language,* Cambridge 1975.

KENNEDY A     *Dramatic Dialogue,* Cambridge 1983.

KOJECKY R     *T S Eliot's Social Criticism,* Faber 1971.

LEAVIS FR     *The Living Principle,* Chatto & Windus 1975.

MOODY AD      *Thomas Stearns Eliot, Poet,* Cambridge 1979.

SMIDT K       *The Importance of Recognition,* Tromso 1973.

SMITH CH      *TS Eliot's Dramatic Theory and Practice,* Princeton University Press 1963.

STYAN JL      *The Dark Comedy,* Cambridge 1968.

WILLIAMS R    *Drama from Ibsen to Eliot,* Chatto & Windus 1952, revised in Penguin 'Peregrine' 1964 to which references relate.

WILLIAMS R    *Drama in Performance,* CA Watts 1968; Penguin 1972 to which references relate.

WILLIAMS R    *Drama from Ibsen to Brecht,* Chatto & Windus 1968; Penguin 1973 to which references relate.

WORTH K       'Eliot and the Living Theatre' in *Eliot in Perspective,* Ed CG Martin, Macmillan 1970.

WORTH K       *The Irish Drama of Europe from Yeats to Beckett,* Athlone Press 1978.

## III THEATRICAL BACKGROUND

BROWNE EM & H *Two in One,* Cambridge 1981.

de MARLEY D     *Costume on the Stage 1600-1940,* Batsford 1982.

DUKES A     *The Scene is Changed,* Macmillan 1942.

MacCARTHY D     *Drama,* Putnam 1940; The Bodley Head.

REDGRAVE M     *The Actor's Ways and Means,* Heinemann 1953.

REDGRAVE M     *In My Mind's Eye,* Weidenfield & Nicholson 1983; Hodder & Stoughton, Coronet 1984.

SPRIGGE E     *Sybil Thorndyke Casson,* Gollancz 1971.

STANISLAVSKY C *Building a Character* (trans. E R Hapgood) Reinhardt 1950. Methuen 1968.

## IV BIOGRAPHICAL

ACKROYD P     *TS Eliot,* Hamish Hamilton 1984.

GORDON L     *Eliot's Early Years,* Oxford 1977.

SENCOURT R     *TS Eliot: a memoir,* ed D Adamson, London 1974. References to Delta Publishing edition, New York 1973.

# NOTES

## I CRITICAL INTRODUCTION

| 1 | Leavis | Ch 3, section on *East Coker,* especially pp 203, 205, 214. |
|---|---|---|
| 2 | Gaskell | Ch 4, p 53; Ch 12, pp 136, 138. |
| 3 | Styan | Ch 4, esp. p 164. |
| 4 | Donoghue | Ch 6. |
| 5 | Jones | Ch 4, esp. pp 106, 110. |
| 6 | Moody | Ch 7, 172-181; esp pp 173, 179, |
| 7 | Harris | See Bibliography |
| 8 | Eliot 'P & D' | 82-4 |
| 9 | Eliot | in an unpublished letter to Brother George Every, 28th March 1939. |
| 10 | Smidt | Ch 5, 75-77. |
| 11 | Eliot | *Religious Drama: Medieval and Modern,* New York 1954 –Detail in a letter about the address which the publishers include in their introduction to this reprint from UNIVERSITY OF EDINBURGH JOURNAL (Autumn 1937) |
| 12 | Browne | |
| 13 | Kennedy | *Six Dramatists* and *Dramatic Dialogue:* |

The earlier of these books contains Kennedy's analysis of the confessional duologue in Eliot; the later book gives the fuller account of such duologue in Ibsen. Since the arguments in the two books complement each other on this point it has seemed to me reasonable to handle them as if they are one.

| 14 | Kennedy 'DD' | Ch 4, 168-80. |
|---|---|---|
| 15 | Kennedy 'SD' | Ch 2, 116-123. |

| 16 | 'FR' Coghill | 12-13. |
| 17 | Eliot | Introduction to *Savonarola*. |
| 18 | Eliot 'RD: M&M' | 11 |
| 19 | Dukes | Ch 3. |
| 20 | MacCarthy | 123ff; 85. |
| 21 | Stanislavsky | 113. |
| 22 | Worth | 158-161 'Eliot and the Living Theatre' in *Eliot in Perspective,* ed. CG Martin, Macmillan 1970. |

## II MARY

| 1 | Browne | 122. |
| 2 | 'FR' Coghill | 196-7 |
| 3 | Browne | 107 |
| 4 | Browne | 117 |
| 5 | Browne | 117-22 |
| 6 | Browne | 107 |
| 7 | Browne | 120 |
| 8 | Eliot 'P and D' | 77 |
| 9 | Browne | 107 |

## II Appendix

| 1 | Browne | 117-22 |
| 2 | Browne | 119 (and in later draft, 96) |
| 3 | Eliot 'T.T.V.O.P' | 91 |
| 4 | Eliot 'TR' | 9 |
| 5 | Eliot, 'T.T.V.O.P' | 89 |
| 6 | Browne | 97 |
| 7 | Donoghue | Ch 6 |
| 8 | Eliot 'R.A.P.D.' | 39 |

## III AGATHA AND AMY

| 1 | 'FR' Coghill | 181 |
| 2 | | Idea worked out in more detail in Harris. |

3   'FR' Coghill      224
4   Jones            106


## IV THE UNCLES AND AUNTS

1   Jones            93
2   'FR' Coghill     182


## V HARRY AND AGATHA

1   'FR' Coghill     216


## VI THE EFFECT ON AMY AND MARY OF HARRY'S DEPARTURE

1   Donoghue         Ch 6
2   Browne           139


## VII UNDER COMPULSION OF WHAT EXPERIENCE...?

1                    Unpublished letter to George Bell, 6 April 1939. Bell Papers 208, f.33 Lambeth Palace Library.
2   Eliot 'P and D'
3                    Unpublished letter to Brother George Every, 28 March 1939.
4   Eliot 'H.A.H.P'  144-6.
5   Ackroyd          246
6                    In an unpublished article on the Plutocrat Scene in *The Rock* G E Evans argues that this episode is a successful 'stage image' of TSE's concern during the 1930s that nominally Christian Britain was too materialistic to present a viable stand against rising Communism and Fascism.

| | | |
|---|---|---|
| 7 | Gordon | See Bibliography |
| 8 | Ackroyd | See Bibliography |
| 9 | Ackroyd | 91 |
| 10 | Ackroyd | 70-1 |
| 11 | Ackroyd | 91 quotes Vivienne Eliot's diary |
| 12 | Ackroyd | 91 |
| 13 | Gordon | 74 |
| 14 | Ackroyd | 65 |
| 15 | Gordon | 124 |
| 16 | Ackroyd | 65 |
| 17 | Gordon | 83 |
| 18 | Gordon | 104 & Ackroyd 111 |
| 19 | Ackroyd | 110 |
| 20 | Ackroyd | 110 |
| 21 | Gordon | 124 |
| 22 | Ackroyd | 159 |
| 23 | Ackroyd | 233 |
| 24 | Ackroyd | 246 |
| 25 | | Martin Tucker,letter to THE TIMES LITERARY SUPPLEMENT, 30 March 1984. Comments on an article by Brigid O'Donovan, 'The Love Song of TS Eliot's Secretary', CONFRONTATION, the literary journal of Long Island University, No 11 Fall/Winter 1975. |
| 26 | Ackroyd | 206 & Sencourt 52 |
| 27 | Sencourt | 197 |
| 28 | Ackroyd | 206 |
| 29 | Ackroyd | 206-7 |
| 30 | Gordon | 129 |
| 31 | Ackroyd | 202 |
| 32 | Ackroyd | 202 |
| 33 | Gordon | 129 & Ackroyd 150 |
| 34 | | Anne Ridler,letter to THE TIMES LITERARY SUPPLEMENT, 13 April 1984 – in response to Martin Tucker (see note 25 above). |
| 35 | Gordon | 74 |
| 36 | Gordon | 94 |
| 37 | Eliot 'F.L.A.' | Preface |

38  Sencourt        Chapter 10
    Gordon          130-1
    Ackroyd         162
39  Gordon          97

Also of interest is the play by Michael Hastings, *Tom and Viv.*
In performance at the Royal Court Theatre, Vivienne was seen
behind a partition trying to get a view into the church. This is a
dramatic licence but strikingly makes the point about her
exclusion from this key decision in TSE's life. See photograph,
THE TIMES 9 February 1984.

40  Gordon          132
41  Eliot           Letter to Paul Elmer More, 3 August
                    1929, quoted Kojecky 73-4


# VIII A MATTER OF FORM AND PERFORMANCE

1   Williams 'D.I.P.'      136
2   Williams 'D.I.P.'      143
3   Williams 'D.F.I.T.E' 268
4   Williams 'D.F.I.T.B' 204-10
5   ibid                   206
6   ibid                   206
7   ibid                   206
8   Eliot 'P and D'        84
9   ibid
10  Browne                 136
11  Williams 'D.I.P.'      142
12                         Eliot in unpublished letter to
                           Brother George Every, 28 March
                           1939.
13                         See photograph, THEATRE
                           WORLD, May 1939 Vol XXXI, No.
                           172
14  Browne & Browne 165
15                         Stella Mary Newton letter to GEE, 4
                           November 1986

Stella Newton designed the original costumes for *The Rock,
Murder in the Cathedral* and *The Family Reunion* and the set for the
post-war revival of *The Family Reunion* at the Mercury
Theatre.

16   ibid
17                          THE TIMES, 1 Nov 1946
18   Browne            117
19                          Stella Newton to GEE, 4 November
                            1986
20   Browne            117
21                          Stella Newton to GEE, 4 November
                            1986
22                          Stella Newton to GEE, 3 July 1980
     See also de Marley, Chapter 7 (p.153 particularly) for
discussion and illustrations of Stella Newton's work for TSE's
plays. A couple of inaccuracies should be noted however:
John Gielgud did *not*, in the end co-direct *The Family Reunion*
with Martin Browne; the picture on 154 is of the post-war
Mercury revival with Stella Newton's setting, not of the
original Westminster Theatre production as stated in the
caption. However, *the costume*, which the illustration is
primarily to show, was identical in both productions.
23                          Stella Newton in conversation with
                            GEE, 1980 and letter 20 September
                            1980.
24   'FR' Coghill       I ii 315
25   Browne            117
26   ibid              136
27   Redgrave 'I.M.M.E' 140 See also Redgrave 'A.W.A.M.',
                            56
28   Redgrave 'I.M.M.E' 140
29   'FR' Coghill       I i 216
30   Browne            137
31   'FR' Coghill       II iii 149
32   ibid              II ii 327ff
33   ibid              II ii 278
34   Worth 'E.A.T.L.T.' 159
35   Redgrave 'I.M.M.E' 141
36   Browne            136
37   Redgrave 'A.W.A.M' 56
38   Williams 'D.I.P.'  142
39   ibid              142
40   ibid              142
41   Williams 'D.F.I.T.E' 268
42                          THE TIMES, 8 June 1956

43 ibid

44 JC Trewin, THE ILLUSTRATED LONDON NEWS, 23 June 1956

45 Michael Elliott's fascination with *The Family Reunion* is reflected in his return to the play for several productions over a period of years in which he worked 'in-the-round':

He worked with a student cast in 1966 and did a production in 1969. Edward Fox played Harry in a further production in 1973 at the Royal Exchange Theatre in Manchester and again at that theatre in March 1979 before transferring to the Round House at Chalk Farm in April. The production then moved to the somewhat different proscenium stage conditions of the Vaudeville Theatre in June.

46 I am indebted here to Professor Katharine Worth's descriptions of the 'in-the-round' student production to be found in 'Eliot and the Living Theatre' and to her comments on the 1969 production in *The Irish Drama of Europe from Yeats to Beckett.*

47 Worth 'E.A.T.L.T.' 159
48 ibid 159
49 Worth 'I.D.D.E.' 206
50 Worth 'E.A.T.L.T.' 159
51 Browne & Browne 167

Also EM Browne's feeling that Michael Elliott had 'solved the problem of the Furies' is referred to in a personal letter to G E E from Pamella Keilly (who was in the original chorus of *Murder in the Cathedral*). She attended the Round House performance of 1979 with E M B. 'In the original production at the Westminster the Furies were grouped centre back – suggesting a bird-like quality and pointing in the direction Harry was to follow. But the stilts and lighting effect at Chalk Farm beat all previous interpretations!' 19 July 1980.

51a  Eliot 'P and D'      82
52   Nicholas de Jongh THE GUARDIAN, 20 June 1979
53   Williams 'D.F.I.T.E'268
54   ibid
55   ibid                 260
56   Eliot 'P and D'      83
57   Worth 'E.A.T.L.T.'161
58   Eliot 'P and D'      82
59   Browne               116
60   'FR' Coghill         II ii 241ff
61   ibid                 I iii 107ff
62   ibid                 I i 189ff
63   Eliot 'A.O.P.D.'     12
64   Williams 'D.I.P'     143-4
65                        *The Family Reunion*, Caedmon TRS
                          308, 1965
66   Sprigge              287-9
67   ibid
68   Williams 'D.I.P.'    144
69                        Personal conversation with GEE
                          1987
70   Eliot 'P and D'      85
71   Eliot 'T.N.F.P.D.'
72                        Robin Thornber, for instance, on the
                          play at The Royal Exchange; THE
                          GUARDIAN, 23 March 1979 –
                          'Theatricality won over the words'
73   Eliot 'P and D'      86
74   Williams 'D.F.I.T.B'206
75   'FR' Coghill         I i 77
76   Williams 'D.F.I.T.B'206
77   ibid                 206-7
78   'FR' Coghill         I i 121
79   ibid                 I i 139
80   Eliot 'P and D'      82
81   Williams 'D.I.P'     118
82   Eliot 'P and D'      73
83                        The phrase is from Harris
84                        Programme note for *The Family
                          Reunion*, Vaudeville Theatre June
                          1979

85   Eliot 'D.O.D.P'      49